# INDIAN LAWS MADE EASY

## BEST-KEPT SECRETS REVEALED

## JOSEPH HENRY MORSETTE MSCJA, JD, LL.M.

IS-PI-MIK-KI-EW HIGH EAGLE

PUBLISHED BY: Joseph Henry Morsette, High Eagle Coaching and Consulting Services, LLC.

DISCLAIMER AND/-OR LEGAL NOTICES

While all attempts have been made to verify information provided in this book and its ancillary materials, neither the author or publisher assumes any responsibility for errors, inaccuracies, or omissions and is not responsible for any financial loss by customer in any manner. Any slights of people or organizations are unintentional. If advice concerning legal, financial, accounting, or related matters is needed, the services of a qualified professional should be sought. This book and its associated ancillary materials, including verbal and written training, is not intended for use as a source of legal, financial, or accounting advice. You should be aware of the various laws governing business transactions or other business practices in your particular geographical location.

EARNINGS & INCOME DISCLAIMER

With respect to the reliability, accuracy, timeliness, usefulness, adequacy, completeness, and/-or suitability of information provided in this book, Joseph Henry Morsette, Joseph Henry Morsette, High Eagle Coaching and Consulting Services, LLC, its partners, associates, affiliates, consultants, and/-or presenters make no warranties, guarantees, representations, or claims of any kind. Readers' results will vary depending on a number of factors. Any and all claims or representations as to include earnings are not to be considered as average earnings. Testimonials are not representative. This book and all products and services are for educational and informational purposes only. Use caution and see the advice of qualified professionals. Check with your accountant, attorney, or professional advisor before acting on this or any information. You agree that Joseph Henry Morsette and/-or Joseph Henry Morsette, High Eagle Coaching and Consulting Services, LLC, is not responsible for the success or failure of your personal, business, health, or financial decisions relating to any information presented by Joseph Henry Morsette, Joseph Henry Morsette, High Eagle Coaching and Consulting Services, LLC, or company products and/-or services. Earnings potential is entirely dependent on the efforts, skills, and application of the individual person. Any examples, stories, references, or case studies are for illustrative purposes only and should not be interpreted as testimonials and/-or examples of what reader and/-or consumers can generally expect from the information. No representation in any part of this information, materials and/-or seminar training are guarantees or promises for actual performance. Any statements, strategies, concepts, techniques, exercises, and ideas in the information, materials and/-

Printed in THE UNITED STATES OF AMERICA

Painting on back cover by Josh Atcheynum "Two Wings/Dancing Buffalo Child." Plains Cree Ledger Artist. Sweetgrass, Saskatchewan, Canada

Cover Design by Tashai Lovington

# WHAT OTHERS ARE SAYING ABOUT JOSEPH HENRY MORSETTE & HIS STRATEGIES

"Joseph Morsette combines theory, critical thinking skills, and practical application whose outcomes can change people's lives. He uses his lived experience in tandem with his professional expertise in creating a method of both personal and academic knowledge to foster positive change for people in their lives."

— **Carma Corcoran**, PhD (Chippewa-Cree) Director-Indian Law, Lewis & Clark Law School, Adjunct Professor, Portland State University. Author of *The Incarceration of Native American Women: Creating Pathways to Wellness and Recovery Through Gentle Action Theory; Gentle Action Theory as a Method of Deliberative Democracy in Addressing the Lack of Voice for Indigenous Students in Institutions of Higher Education;* and *Native Americans – Racism and the Criminal Justice System.*

"Joseph is so encouraging, and inspiring people to live a better life!" — **William Walton**, BA MSc Dip Env Law CPE LLM BVC MJIL MRTPI Barrister of Law (Lincoln's Inn) (Non-Practising) Senior Lecturer in Property Law at Oxford Brookes University in the United Kingdom. [Former MJIL student of mine].

"In the years that I have worked with Joseph, he always exemplified a strong commitment to not only encouraging and inspiring both Native and Non-Native individuals to understand and appreciate and respect the varying cultural differences between and among them as well as strive towards seeking out ways that both can be united in their common goals and striving towards achievement of those goals together. He has always striven to be a 'teacher' and mentor towards creating a sense of community and encouraged those with whom he has worked with an ability to 'think outside the box' in creating tools and strategies that assist in striving towards and obtaining establishing goals."

— **Ruth Hara**, Former Consultant in the area of Tribal Child Support.

"Joseph is a plethora of knowledge of federal Indian law and cases. His understanding of the modern tribal government and its nuances' is truly amazing. This book will truly change the approach that many have concerning tribal law and governance, and be a guiding beacon for many to take to heart, and inspire not only tribal members, but all members of society." — **Rev. Dr. Alexander Louis Medina**, JD, PMP, Director of TALM International, Inc., a non-profit corporation.

"I always appreciated how Joseph passionately answered my questions, made the difficult or complex answers easier to comprehend, and made me want to learn more." — **Rebecca Flanders, J.D.**, UND Alumna, Prosecutor from 2017-2022.

"Joseph helps clarify the ongoing issues in tribal law by doing a detailed deep dive, including many legal references, to help you find the answers you need with shortcuts to this extensive information." — **Theresa Z. DeWit**, #1 Best-Selling Author *Less Conflict – More Joy*, Course Creator, Speaker, and Coach.

"Joseph is so encouraging, and inspiring people to live a better life!" — **Dr. Wayne Fox**, Ph.D., White Shield School District Superintendent; White Shield, ND.

"With all the information Joseph's writings and collection of information, I can see how this could have a great impact for future generations of tribal members, non-member Indian, or the non-Indian. His book helps to define laws and rights of tribal members, which could have a greater impact on their lives in so many positive ways!" — **Veronica May Marsette McCabe**.

"Joseph 'IsPiMikKiEw HighEagle' Morsette – presents a scholarly yet easy to understand academic book filled with powerful strategies, designed to inspire you with concepts, ideas, and proven methods sure to help you. This remarkable resource will give you the foundation you need to understand Indian law, federal Indian law, tribal law, treaties, and more importantly outlines important action steps – 'the best-kept secrets' on how you can maximize your job offers!" — **Pam Courtney**, MNA: graduate studies in nonprofit administration, BSBA, MIT: Management Technology Founder: College Credit by Exam.

"Joseph's style is not only helpful, but educational. His detail, and insights, as well as thorough explanations will empower persons lives!" — **Sandra A. Alicea**, SPED, JD, and Educational Advocate.

"Joseph's passion to bring awareness, justice, and healing to his community by shining light on their history, the path their generations have walked on, the sacrifices, the atrocities, the resilience of their spirits, is very moving for me personally! You will always feel inspired and uplifted in his presence! I strongly recommend this book to everyone who wants to learn about the struggles, successes, and evolution of our native brothers, and sisters! I found the book very educational, and moving!" — **Ritu Rani**, #1 Best-Selling Author, Coach, and Speaker.

"Joseph is so encouraging, and inspiring people to live a better life!" — **Sereda Fowlkes,** Certified Wholistic Health Coach.

"Joseph's concepts, ideas, methods, and outcomes change people's lives!" — **Heather Pelletier**, Compliance Risk Mgr. Grey Eagle Casino, Alberta, Canada.

"Joseph is the smartest person I know. Any information he's willing to share on how to be successful is worth reading. You're bound to learn something new!" — **KiEwSis, Antonio Joseph Morsette**, Co-Host – A Smudge For Your Thoughts.

"Joseph's strategies have the potential to change a person's life if one chooses to open his or her mind to his overall concepts and ways of thinking." — **Chontay Mitchell**, aka Chontay Standing Rock, Singer/Song Writer.

"Native Americans are unique individually. There are different tribes all over the world. We all go through ups and downs in our lives. We all stick together. Joseph is the one of many helping hands in the ups and downs. Tribal law is very complex. Joseph helps dissect it down for everyone, or anyone to understand."
— **Oddessa Kinsel**, Tribal Member of the Dine Nation.

"Joseph has dedicated his career to improve the quality of life and services available to the tribal community. With a vast understanding of the rule of law and using that knowledge to make a stand on Tribal cases. Joseph's strategies have the power to change lives!" — **Evelyn Jimenez**, Attorney.

"Joseph takes the complex subject of Indian laws and boils it down into easy to understand nuggets of information. If you are looking to start or deepen your journey into Indian law and the history of our native brothers and sisters, this is the book for you!"
— **Tashai Lovington** #1 bestselling author of *Fill The Gap: How to Manifest From Where You Are Now to the life You Want*

# MOTIVATE AND INSPIRE OTHERS!

"Share This Book"

Eight Reasons why you should buy this Book in Bulk:

1. **REWARD** those who have helped your group by giving them a FREE autographed book;
2. **INVEST** in your community, your inner circle;
3. **INCREASE ATTENDANCE** by advertising that the first "X" number of people attending your event receive a FREE autographed book;
4. **DOOR PRIZES**: Give the books away as door prizes;
5. **BOOK SIGNING**: Advertise that Joseph will be autographing books after the event to increase attendance;
6. **RAISE MONEY FOR YOUR GROUP** by selling the books at your event for the full retail price;
7. **INCREASE EVENT VALUE** by incorporating the cost of the book for every participant into your registration fee; and
8. **AUTOGRAPH SESSION**: Joseph will conduct a special autograph session to sign all of the books at no cost,

Retail $24.95

## Special Quantity Discounts

5-20 Paperback Books
$21.95 + S&H
21-99 Paperback Books
$18.95 + S&H
100-499 Paperback Books
$15.95 + S&H
500-999 Paperback Books
$10.95 + S&H
1,000+ Paperback Books
$8.95 + S&H

To Place an Order Contact Joseph:
www.HighEagleLLC.com

# THE IDEAL PROFESSIONAL SPEAKER FOR YOUR NEXT EVENT!

Any organization that wants to develop their people to become "extraordinary," needs to hire Joseph for keynote and/-or workshop training!

TO CONTACT, OR BOOK JOSEPH TO SPEAK:
Joseph Henry Morsette,
High Eagle Coaching and Consulting Services, LLC
www.HighEagleLLC.com

I can coach, and teach on the principles, tips, secrets, concepts, and ideas from my book to connect, influence, and impact your life. Some organizational line-items that you may consider, include: [1] Continuing Education Budget; [2] Learning Materials Budget; and/-or [3] Training and Development Budget.

# THE IDEAL CONSULTANT FOR YOU!

If you are ready to overcome challenges, have major breakthroughs, and achieve higher levels, then you will love having Joseph as your consultant!

TO CONTACT, OR BOOK JOSEPH TO CONSULT:
Joseph Henry Morsette,
High Eagle Coaching and Consulting Services, LLC

www.HighEagleLLC.com

# DEDICATION

*It is with great respect, admiration, and sincere appreciation, that I dedicate this book to my wonderful family. To my great-grandparents, my grandparents, my parents, my wife, my children, and my grandchildren.*

*No-tah-wi (my father) Ki-Yu-Stas (Generous Chief of the South), James David Morsette for his teachings. I am grateful for the spiritual and cultural teachings from my family and friends throughout Turtle Island, especially within the communities surrounding Seattle, Washington, and the Rocky Boy's Indian Reservation, Montana.*

*Without you and the lessons you have taught me throughout my life, I would not have the blessings of being where I am today. Thank you from the bottom of my heart! I love you dearly. (Kisahkitin).*

*Sitting is paternal grandmother, Ida Catherine Gardipee Morsette and paternal grandfather, Joseph David Morsette; Standing is uncle Elmer Francis Morsette, and Edward Francis Marsette.*

Grandmother, Ida Catherine Gardipee Morsette, with my son, Antonio Joseph Morsette.

My grandmother and some of my aunties

From left to right: Jeanie Morsette, Alma Morsette, Cohee, grandmother, Ida, Doris Morsette, Gomez, and Delene Wells
[not pictured aunties: Katherine Kate Anderson Spencer (Calgary, Alberta, Canada), Dorothy.
"big auntie" Morsette Almero (Los Angeles, CA), and Virginia "little auntie" Morsette Allery (Los Angeles, CA)].

*My uncles with my father*

*Back row from left to right: Danny Morsette, Sr., Elmer Francis Morsette, Victor Morsette, and Richard Morsette; front row from left to right: Edward Francis Marsette, and my father, James David Morsette.*

*My father and I*

*My mother and I*

*Our father, and his children.*

*top going clockwise: me, Benita, Michael, Sunshine, Calvin, Raven Thunder, and Evie.*

*My wifey Juanita Benally Morsette, and I.*

*Our wedding day, June 16, 2012*

*My father, my daughter Justice, and I*

*Me, Justice, and Juanita*

*Me, my daughter Tiffany, my son Antonio, and my father.*

*Tiffany and Antonio*

*Me, Justice and Antonio.*

*Antonio in his traditional regalia*

*Justice in her Jingle Dress regalia*

# CONTENTS

# FOREWORD

I am Monique Vondall-Rieke, a member of the Turtle Mountain Band of Chippewa Indians, who reside in north central North Dakota. I have worked in tribal law and policy for several years, served as appellate justice for my tribe's court of appeals and currently live in Alaska. I have been a training and technical assistance provider for tribal courts since I attended the University of North Dakota School of Law, where I met Joseph Morsette in the Fall of 2001. It was the year of 9/11 and the first year of law school for us both. Joseph, who was enlisted in the Air National Guard at that time, was called to duty and put his life and future on hold for our nation. At the time we were both single parents.

I wholeheartedly believe that Joseph is the author who is best to achieve your knowledge of Indian Law and how to learn it in an easy and quick way. Joseph's book is a valuable quick way to navigate Indian Country and the laws that govern. This book is a powerful guide for any lay person or Indian Law encounter across the nation. Joseph's strategies have the power to save lives!

Joseph himself has served in multiple tribal judge positions, conducts trainings and has been a shining example of a successful and resourceful legal professional. His military history has built his disciplined and traditional method of approaching Indian Law and his willingness to share that in this remarkable book with those who are fortunate to possess it is exemplary of his dedication to educating on this topic.

My recommendation is that you keep this great resource handy if you work in any capacity with Indian Law issues or even are a novice reader of Indian Country!

Monique Vondall-Rieke, JD

# A MESSAGE TO YOU!

I set out to write this book to serve you. [1] I want to help you the tribal lay advocate with little to no education and/-or experience achieve more wins for your clients in tribal courts without having to stress about getting new clients. [2] I want to help you the college student maximize job offers as you transition into the tribal government office. [3] I want to help you the attorney with some, or no experience in federal Indian law, tribal governments and law achieve more wins for your clients in tribal, state, and federal courts. And [4] I want to help you achieve a better understanding in what is federal Indian law, versus what is tribal law, and the structure of what is tribal government, and the laws that impact you when you enter Indian country.

I was once a tribal college student, a lay advocate in tribal court, a federal Bureau of Indian Affairs police officer, a tribal trial court Associate and Chief judge, a tribal appellate court justice, a tribal public defender, a tribal prosecutor, inside legal counsel to a tribal business committee, inside legal counsel to a tribal legislative branch, and a legal consultant for several tribes, a U.S. Army National Guardsman; Active Duty U.S. Air Force, and Air National Guardsman police officer.

I am now reaching back in time, metaphorically speaking to help you how I learned federal Indian law, tribal government, and the laws that impact all peoples on tribal territories. I am sharing with you what has worked for me, and how I got over the metaphorical bridge to success. It is almost like having a condensed version of a Felix Cohen's Handbook (the Bible of federal Indian law) at your side. I am further sharing with you my personal family stories, and my personal experiences. If you choose to apply the principles in this book, you too can find success in your life.

I am empowering your beliefs with strategies, concepts, ideas, methods, and positive outcomes. I want to help you on your own heroes' journey. Taking you from where you are right now, to where you want to ultimately be. The truth is, people want to learn from someone who has been through it already, and gotten a new result. I am taking decades of my personal education, along with my personal experiences, and compressing a timeline of decades into days for you into this short easy to read book.

People are hungry to learn from someone with a specific knowledge. If you choose to apply the principles in this book, you will literally download, and condense decades of data, and learn in days what took others years to learn. I will share with you my personal stories, a glimpse of what is possible from someone who was there to where I wanted to go. Armed with this specific knowledge, I can help thrust you over the metaphorical bridge, get past the mess, the uncomfortable actions; into a positive solution, of skill, of mastery, and of purpose. For example, helping you to think differently being learned in tribal government and laws that impact all peoples on tribal territories.

After each chapter, I am ethically persuading you to take action on something that could change your life for the better. This is my gift to you, through the power of having written a book; along with other helpful resources for you, such as mentorship programs; online courses; and speaking engagements.

I once walked in your shoes, and sat where you are sitting at a tribal college, particularly, Stone Child College. The original campus was in the Agency Area on the Rocky Boy's Indian Reservation. I was awarded the Tribal Academic Bridge Scholarship to the University of

Great Falls, and enrolled in their criminal justice, law enforcement concentration online Bachelor of Science Degree Program.

What does this mean for you? It does not matter where you came from in life. Always look to where you want to be, and go for it. You can achieve anything in life, if you set your mind to it. Having the right mindset is key. I want to help you gain a better understanding of the material in this book. And together we can. I will share with you my many years of education, and real-world work experience. I want to lift you up, and move you forward, as you become more knowledgeable and thinking differently learned in tribal government and laws that impact all peoples on tribal territories.

After reading this book, regardless, of whether you are a tribal member, a non-member Indian, or a non-Indian, you will have a better understanding, and be more confident in the subject matter of what is Indian law, what are the differences between federal Indian law, and tribal law; and have more knowledge in your general understanding of what is tribal government and laws that impact all peoples on tribal territories; and have more specific knowledge in your general understanding of what is tribal government, and laws that impact all persons on the Rocky Boy's Indian Reservation.

There are, as of the publication of this text, 574 federally recognized American Indian and Alaska Native tribal nations in the United States. The Little Shell Tribe of Chippewa Indians of Montana was recognized by Act of Congress (December 2019). [See Bureau of Indian Affairs, Indian Entities Recognized by and Eligible to Receive Services from the United States Bureau of Indian Affairs, 87 Fed. Reg. 4636-4641].

Although there are a lot of similarities between each tribal nation, each tribal nation is unique in their own ways. Each tribal nation has their own unique oral, legal, and political histories, ceremonies, languages, customs, traditions, values, beliefs, norms, structures, practices, and laws.

Series Editor's Forward

INDIAN LAWS MADE EASY - BEST-KEPT SECRETS REVEALED
Indian Laws Made Easy Best-Kept Secrets Revealed series is

designed in part for Tribal Colleges, and Universities to provide you with the necessary tools to become learned in modern tribal governments, and the laws that impact all peoples on tribal territories. Throughout this series, you will begin to develop your skills, and identify similarities, and differences between other tribal governments, and identify what government actor(s) are doing (federal, state, and/-or tribe); what laws the actor(s) are applying either exclusive jurisdiction, or concurrent jurisdiction (federal, state, and/-or tribe); and identify who the person is (you), either as the tribal member, the non-member Indian, or the non-Indian.

In this first book, in Chapter 1, you will examine – How to become learned in Indian law. In Chapter 2, you will examine – How to become learned in tribal government and law. And, in Chapter 3, you will examine – How to become learned in the tribal government and laws that impact the Rocky Boy's Indian Reservation. A closer look at one tribal community, from the early years to contemporary times, and viewing their legal documents.

# CHAPTER 1
# HOW TO BECOME
# LEARNED IN INDIAN LAW

## WHAT IS INDIAN LAW?

When you speak of Indian law, you are talking about federal Indian law. What I like to call "Instruments of Cultural Oppression. This means the collection, or body of Treaties; Congressional Statutes; Presidential (POTUS) Executive Orders; federal departments, and agencies regulations, promulgated rules, police and procedures; and common law doctrines of the Supreme Court (SCOTUS), along with the lower federal court cases decided under federal law that regulates the relationship among federal, state, and tribal governments, individual Indians, and non-Indians within tribal territories, and communities.

Indian law is really Fifth Amendment law to the United States Constitution. [See Amendment 5 of the U.S. Constitution (1791) Criminal actions – Provisions concerning – Due process of law and just compensation clauses].

"NO person shall be held to answer for a capital, or otherwise infamous crime, unless on a presentment or indictment of a Grand Jury, except in cases arising in the land or naval forces, or in the Militia, when in actual service in time of War or public danger; nor shall any person be subject for the same offense to be twice put in jeopardy of life or limb; nor shall be compelled in any criminal case to be a witness against himself, nor be deprived of life, liberty, or property, without due process of law; nor shall private property be taken for the public use, without just compensation."

## WHO IS AN INDIAN DEFINED FOR FEDERAL JURISDICTION?

To be considered an Indian, one generally has to have both "a significant degree of blood and sufficient connection to their tribe to be regarded [by the tribe or the government] as one of its members for criminal JX purposes. [*See U.S. v. Rogers 45 U.S. 567, 573 (1846), the Racialization of Indian Law in the 19TH Century, Rogers weaponized Worcester); also see U.S. v. Torres 733 F.2d 449, 455 (7TH Cir. 1984)*].

Tribal membership can generally be established through the Department of Interior, Bureau of Indian Affairs, or tribal enrollment office and records. Enrollment has NOT been held to be an absolute requirement for federal JX. [*See U.S. v. Antelope 430 U.S. 641, 647 n.7 (1977)*].

If a person is NOT enrolled nor eligible for enrollment in a U.S. federally recognized tribe, then they are probably NOT an Indian for criminal jurisdictional purposes. Persons who are NOT members of federally recognized tribes in the U.S., do NOT have a special legal relationship with the U.S. government. The Supreme Court of the United States (SCOTUS) held that Indians can be treated differently under the law, NOT because of their race or ancestry, but because of their unique political status under federal law. [*See Morton v. Mancari, 417 U.S. 535 (1974); and U.S. v. Antelope, 430 U.S. 641 (1977)*].

Canadian First Nations Indigenous Peoples are NOT federally acknowledged by the U.S. government; and therefore, it has been held that their members are NOT to be treated as Indians, either as perpetrators or as victims, under 18 U.S.C. §1152 – the general crimes act; nor under 18 U.S.C. §1153 – the Indian major crimes act.

## WHAT IS INDIAN COUNTRY DEFINED?

To be recognized as Indian country, the land must either be within the exterior boundaries of an Indian reservation or it must be trust land, that is held by the U.S. federal government for the specific tribe or tribal member.

18 U.S.C. §1151 – Indian country defined.

This is actually a criminal statute. It is applied in criminal and in civil cases.

[a] All land within reservations.

All land within the limits of any Indian reservation under the JX of the U.S. government notwithstanding the issuance of any patent, and including rights-of-way running through the reservation;

[NOTE: Reserved Lands, now Reservations were created by Treaty, Statute, and Executive Order].

[b] All dependent Indian communities.

All dependent Indian communities within the borders of the U.S. whether within the original or subsequently acquired territory thereof, and whether within or without the limits of a state; and

[NOTE: See *U.S. v. Sandoval, 231 U.S. 28 (1913); U.S. v. McGowan, 302 U.S. 535 (1938); Alaska v. Native Village of Venetie, 522 U.S. 520 (1998)*].

[c] All Indian allotments.

All Indian allotments, the Indian title to which have NOT been extinguished, including rights-of-way running through the same (on and off reservation).

[NOTE:] Primarily from 1887 up to 1934, the federal government ran programs where some parcels of tribal trust land were allotted or assigned to particular Indian persons, or particular Indian families. Many parcels of land are still in restricted, or trust status.

## THE TREATY ERA

1492. Inherent Retained Diminished Sovereignty.

The colonial period began with the coming of the Spanish to the southwest and the French, English, and Dutch to the east coast. While Columbus arrived in 1492 in what would later become the settler, colonizer, the United States. American Indian and Alaska Native populations in this area known as Turtle Island were largely undisturbed for the next 200 years. For most of the 1700s, American

Indian tribes still controlled trade, and the trade routes. Many Tribes played the colonial powers off against one another, and kept a balance of power as successful military forces.

1790-1834. Complete federal pre-emption over Indian affairs.

Sections 1 through 6 of the Trade and Intercourse Act. The Act to regulate Trade and Intercourse with the Indian tribes, which came from the 1763 British Proclamation.

## PEACE TREATIES – LAND CESSION TREATIES

During the American Revolution, for example, the Seneca fought on the side of the British, the Oneida signed a treaty of neutrality, and the Delaware signed a treaty of alliance with the Revolutionary government. When the war ended and the British pulled back to what is now the Canadian border, the Seneca were still in military control of most of New York State. The U.S. signed a peace treaty with the Seneca. These treaties firmly established a government-to-government relationship and affirmed the sovereignty of Tribes. Framers of the U.S. Constitution built these concepts into the founding documents of the U.S., declaring Indian tribes to be "dependent nation states" and giving Congress the right to regulate the relationships between Tribes, and States, setting up the framework of federal Indian policy.

They entered into treaties with tribes just as they did with other European countries. Tribal sovereignty is recognized by:

- Up to 400 + treaties signed by POTUS, ratified by 2/3 of the U.S. Senate with Indian tribes up to 1871.
- These treaties have never been repealed; mostly NOT enforced. And these treaties ceded land in exchange for U.S. protection, health, shelter, food, clothing, etc.
- NOTE: Treaty with the U.S. is very sensitive with treaty tribes.
- Executive Orders are at the pleasure of POTUS.
- Congressional Statutes after 1871 [(100 Senators) and (435 House of Representatives)].

Many tribes bargained away their inherent authority when they signed treaties. Some examples include Treaties with Cherokee (military alliance, peace treaties after a fight, then negotiating the meets and bounds of a reservation, land cession treaties, removal treaties (aka the trail of tears), reservation establishment treaties) [Art. 5, 7 Stat. 481 (1835)]; Choctaws & Chickasaws [Art. 7, 11 Stat. 703 (1856)]; Creeks & Seminoles [Art. 15, 11 Stat. 703 (1856)]: specifically granted the right of self-government to the tribes [but] specifically excluded JX over nonmembers. Termination treaties, winding down the government-to-government relationship.

Each tribe has a unique history in terms of interaction with colonists and historical relationships with the U.S. government. Equally true is the fact that tribal customs, traditions, and notions of justice vary greatly among the more than 574 federally recognized and state recognized tribes in the United States.

- The United States would ultimately win out over all other European Colonizer Nation States:
- (EX) British/United States conquest/Indian Removal Act of 1830.
- Spanish/Mexico/southwest conquest/United States.
- French/United States/Louisiana purchase.
- Russia/United States/Alaskan purchase.

The question of Tribal sovereignty emerged in the early 1800's in a trilogy of cases commonly referred to as "The Marshall Trilogy." Although these cases were rooted in territorial discussions one question that the Supreme Court of the United States (SCOTUS) addressed was the political status of tribes within the U.S. In addressing this issue, SCOTUS drew upon international principles of law to ultimately find that tribes were in fact self-governing; however, SCOTUS determined that the self-governance of tribes in the U.S. had been diminished. Although legal scholars have criticized SCOTUS' application of international law, the holdings of SCOTUS from the trilogy remain the primary backdrop for tribal sovereignty and ultimately for the political status that tribes now possess within the U.S.

The holdings in these three major SCOTUS cases resulted in a determination that the political status of tribes was that of "domestic dependent nations." SCOTUS when on to find that tribes possess inherent rights of self-governance, subject to divestiture by the United States federal government. Another way of stating this premise is that tribes maintain all "inherent" rights of a sovereign NOT otherwise extinguished by the U.S. Congress through treaty or legislative act.

In a legal and governmental context sovereignty can be defined as the absolute and independent right to make one's own laws, rules, or regulations, and be governed by the same. To this end, tribal governments retain this same absolute right to make laws and to be governed by them, subject only to the plenary power of the U.S. federal government. Tribes are thus trying to delicately balance the management of their own affairs with the scrutiny of outside jurisdictions, a difficult balance knowing that federal assertion of plenary power could, at any time, interfere with that exercise.

## THE POWER OF CHIEF JUSTICE JOHN MARSHALL'S PEN AT A GLANCE

The Constitution (1787) said about the power of the Supreme Court:

### Article III, Section 1

The judicial Power of the United States, shall be vested in one supreme Court, and in such inferior Courts as the Congress may from time to time ordain and establish…

John Marshall wrote about the power of the Supreme Court

*Marbury v. Madison, 5 U.S. 137 (1803).* The Supreme Court has the power to declare acts of Congress void for being "repugnant to" the Constitution, what we now call "unconstitutional."

*Fletcher v. Peck, 10 U.S. 87 (1810).* The Supreme Court has the power to declare state laws unconstitutional.

The Constitution said about Indians:

. . .

**Article I, Section 2**

The House of Representatives shall be composed of Members chosen every second Year by the People of the several States...

Representatives and direct Taxes shall be apportioned among the several States which may be included within this Union, according to their respective Numbers, which shall be determined by adding to the whole Number of free Persons, including those bound to Service for a Term of Years, and excluding Indians NOT taxed, three fifths of all other Persons.

**Article I, Section 8**

The Congress shall have Power...To regulate Commerce with foreign Nations, and among the several States, and with the Indian Tribes.

John Marshall wrote about Indians:

The Marshall Trilogy Cases: (Johnson; Cherokee Nation; and Worcester).

## 1823. JOHNSON V. MCINTOSH, 21 U.S. 543 (1823)

Tribal Authority versus Federal Authority

- Facts: Johnson bought land from the Illinois Tribe in 1773, before the United States became an independent nation. Decades later and after the U.S. had become independent, another man, McIntosh, bought the exact same land from the U.S. government.
- Issue: Who owned the land?
- Holding: McIntosh according to SCOTUS, which based its decision on the principle of International Law, "to the victor belongs the spoils." Europeans had established the doctrine of discovery, which gave title to those who "discovered" it. The only concession the court made for the tribe was to be certain they had been adequately compensated. SCOTUS then said that the rulers of the old world "made ample

compensation to the inhabitant of the new, by bestowing
upon them civilization and Christianity."

- Private citizens could NOT purchase lands from Native
  Americans. Indians do NOT own the land beneath their feet,
  but rather have a right of occupancy that may be
  extinguished by the U.S. This is based on the Doctrine of
  Discovery, understood to mean the right of Christians to take
  the property of non-Christians.
- The Doctrine of Discovery incorporates the International
  Rule of Discovery. Acquires this right from Great Britain. By
  Treaty, Act of War, By Abandonment.

TAKEAWAYS

Heartbreaking, racist, immoral, and one of the most reviled
decisions in all of Indian law. Theft and dispossession of Indian lands.
Limits Indian tribes to occupancy and only selling Indian title to the
U.S. federal government. Aboriginal title, title that has never been
ceded, or sold in any way, or alienated to a non-Indian government.
Doctrine of Discovery. U.S. has the exclusive right over all other
European Nations to acquire Native lands. Acquire through: [1]
Purchase (ex) U.S. purchased the Louisiana purchase from France in
1803; and (ex) U.S. purchased Alaska from Russia in 1867; or [2]
Conquest. NOTE: This case stands as a reaffirmation of federal plenary
power over Indian affairs.

## THE REMOVAL ERA

The Five Civilized Tribes, aka (the Five Tribes): the Cherokee, Choctaw
(1833 removal treaty), Chickasaw (1833 removal treaty), Seminole, and
Creek were all about protecting their tribal treaty rights. Their
ancestral lands were east of the Mississippi River. They were forcibly
removed to modern day eastern territories, to what is now the state of
Oklahoma.

Other tribes such as woodland and great lakes Indians (the

Anishanaabe story of harvesting corn, bean, and squash – the three sisters) were removed from now occupied states that included, but were not limited to: Minnesota, New York, Michigan, Ohio, Indiana, and Illinois, and were forced to assimilate onto the plains of what is now states such as Montana, Kansas, and Oklahoma. Tribal members were granted American citizenship in part, because they owned land, they paid taxes, were Christianized, and often gave up their tribal treaty rights.

NOTE: In ancient Greek, you were either a citizen, or you were a slave. A citizen is someone who owns slaves. Citizens of the Five Tribes, owned slaves up until the end of the U.S. civil war. There are at least 10,000 descendants of Freedmen enrolled in the Cherokee Nation of Oklahoma.

## 1831. *CHEROKEE NATION V. GEORGIA, 30 U.S. 1 (1831)*

Tribal Authority versus State Authority.

- Facts: In 1802, the U.S. federal government promised Cherokee lands to Georgian settlers. The Cherokee people had historically occupied the lands in Georgia and been promised ownership through a series of treaties, including the Treaty of Holston in 1791. Between 1802 and 1828, land-hungry settlers and politicians attempted to negotiate with the Cherokee people in order to claim the land for themselves.
- In 1828, tired of resistance and emboldened by the election of Andrew Jackson (a president in favor of removal of Indigenous peoples), members of the Georgia state legislature passed a series of laws meant to strip the Cherokee people of their rights to the land. In defense of the Cherokee people, Principle Chief John Ross and attorney William Wirt asked the Court to grant an injunction to prevent the laws from going into effect.
- Issue: Does SCOTUS have JX to grant an injunction against Georgia laws that would harm the Cherokee people under

Article III of the U.S. Constitution, which gives the Court JX over cases "between a State or the citizens thereof, and foreign states, citizens, or subjects?" Do the Cherokee people constitute a foreign state?

- Holding: SCOTUS held that it did NOT have JX to hear the case because the Cherokee Nation is NOT a "foreign State" but rather a "domestic foreign state," as defined by Article III of the Constitution. The Cherokee Nation was NOT a foreign nation, nor a state, but a domestic dependent nation, with a relationship to the U.S. like that of a "ward to its guardian." Indian nations are NOT foreign states that can bring lawsuits in the Supreme Court, but rather "domestic dependent nations."

Holding: SCOTUS held that it did NOT have JX to hear the case because the Cherokee Nation is NOT a "foreign State" but rather a "domestic foreign state," as defined by Article III of the Constitution. The Cherokee Nation was NOT a foreign nation, nor a state, but a domestic dependent nation, with a relationship to the U.S. like that of a "ward to its guardian." Indian nations are NOT foreign states that can bring lawsuits in the Supreme Court, but rather "domestic dependent nations."

TAKEAWAYS

Domestic Dependent Nation = Ward/Guardianship Relationship Trust (status). NOT foreign nation. NOT a foreign state. [1] Limited sovereignty; [2] Resembles Guardianship/ward relationship with the U.S. government; [3] Excludes state intervention; [4] What has NOT already been taken away remains (the reserved rights doctrine). Modern day Trust Doctrine.

## 1832. *WORCESTER V. GEORGIA, 31 U.S. (6 PET.) 515 (1832)*

(The supposedly "Good Indian Law" case) (the most cited pre-civil war case). State Authority versus Federal Authority.

- Facts: Georgia felt state law should override federal, and set out to prove it b establishing a series of laws including that no one could enter the Cherokee Reservation without a permit from the state. A minister, Sam Worcester, had been invited to the reservation by a number of Cherokees, and went in without a permit that was supposed to be issued by the state of Georgia (according to the state of Georgia), and was arrested, charged, and imprisoned for four and a half years.
- Issue: State Authority versus Federal Authority.
- Holding: Worcester won, SCOTUS ruled the "Cherokee Nation, then, is a distinct community, occupying its own territory, with boundaries accurately described, in which the laws of Georgia can have NO force, and the citizens of Georgia have NO right to enter, but with the assent of the Cherokees themselves, or in conformity with treaties and with the acts of Congress. State law shall have NO force in Indian country. This case laid out the relationship between tribes and the states, and the federal government, stating that the federal government was the sole authority to deal with Indian nations.
- Citing to the U.S. Constitution; non-Intercourse Acts; Treaties. Federal Courts, NOT state courts. To protect Indian tribes from other governmental entities, particularly the states' encroachment. The laws of Georgia shall have NO force in Indian country, subject to federal review.

TAKEAWAYS

Indian tribes have traditionally had power "over both their members and their territory." Therefore, a tribe could exercise power over non-Indians and non-member Indians who entered reservation land. SCOTUS held that Georgia law had NO effect in Cherokee Country even in the case of non-Indians. The history of tribal self-government forms the basis for the exercise of modern powers. Indian tribes consistently have been recognized, first by the European nations. SCOTUS also held that the U.S. in Congress assembled, shall have the sole and exclusive right of regulating the trade with the Indian tribes and managing all their affairs [Indian Commerce Clause Article 1, Section 8, Clause 3]. Congress is the appropriate body to deal with Indian Nations, NOT states. Plenary Power Doctrine: Complete, total authority. Excludes state authority. Limited Judicial involvement. The Legislative power of the state is limited to citizens within the legislative body's involvement. NOTE: POTUS Jackson implemented the [voluntary] Indian Removal Act (1830) by forcing the five civilized tribes to leave their ancestral homelands and march to present day Oklahoma.

YOU must cite Worcester when discussing Indian Rights. Limits the Doctrine of Discovery. McLean's Concurrence: The Rule is fine to him, but there needed to be an opening for state's authority to take over when the Indians die out.

NOTE: In an ironic twist, Congress' failure to discharge the obligations imposed by plenary power, combined with the authority that spins out of MARBURY, has laid the most odious recent colonial usurpations of federal Indian law at the door NOT of Congress, the possessor of the power, but of SCOTUS, the creator of it.

## THE FOUR FUNDAMENTALS OF THE MARSHALL MODEL:

1. PLENARY POWER DOCTRINE. Belongs exclusively to Congress. Seems to be very broad. Federal power is plenary, and exclusive to deal with Indian tribes. Excludes the states. States do NOT have power in Indian affairs, absent delegation from Congress. [See PL-280]. Limited Judicial involvement.

2. DIMINISHED SOVEREIGNTY PRINCIPLE. Indian tribes are inherently sovereign. They do NOT derive their sovereignty from the U.S. Constitution. They derive their sovereignty from within their own Indian tribes. The tribes possess all the powers that a nation possess, until they come under the duty of protection by the U.S., and negotiate what they

scope of their powers are. Domestic Dependent Nation (status). As for the Indians from the Calvin's case, while Calvin can bring a case in the English Court, Infidels cannot. The normal rule: Indians have NO rights. If the King does NOT recognize them, they do NOT exist. Furthermore, if Congress does NOT recognize them, they do NOT exist. Therefore, under the Doctrine of Discovery, the Indian Tribes have DIMINISHED SOVEREIGNTY (the Diminished Sovereignty Principle). NOTE: Indians need Congress to protect their sovereignty rights.

3. TRUST RELATIONSHIP (DOCTRINE). The Trust Doctrine created by SCOTUS. Originally was called the "Duty of Protection," pursuant to customary international law. The federal government as the Guardian, takes the Indian tribes as their Ward, and brings them under their umbrella of protection. Indians are in a state of pupilage, now called the Trust Doctrine. The U.S. has a greater level of responsibility. (EX) Trust relationship by the federal government over all of Indians and their affairs; such as education, health, food, security, governance, etc. Examples of the Trust Responsibility: *Cobell* Litigation. Executive agencies are responsible for implementing Congressional treaties, and statutes. [*See Morton v. Mancari, (1974)*]. NOT racial discrimination, but a political classification as a member of a federally recognized Indian tribe. Minimum baseline on the duty of protection. See United Nations Declaration on the rights of Indigenous Peoples (2007).

4. CANONS OF CONSTRUCTION. When interpreting Treaties and/-or Statutes. Procedural canons of construction – Indians are being/acting like Indians. Interpret treaties under adhesion contract law, [1] Ambiguous expressions must be resolved in favor of the Indian parties concerned; [2] Indian treaties must be interpreted as the Indians themselves would have understood them; and [3] Indian treaties must be liberally construed in favor of the Indians. NOTE: Until Congress expressly takes it away in clear and expressly

stated language, it remains, until it is exactly on point to take it away, it remains. Examples of Canons of Construction: Fishing Treaties. Bolt decision; Mille Lacs decision. Both using the canons of construction and upholding tribal rights. 1888. Fort Belknap Indian Community. Left out of water rights. Reserved Water Rights Doctrine, applying the cannons of construction.

## THE FOUR CHARACTERISTICS OF THE MARSHALL MODEL CASE:

1. You do NOT question the Doctrine of Discovery;
2. The State's power of the Doctrine of Discovery is grounded in the Doctrine of Discovery;
3. The Court's racist character can be found through usage, image, stereotype, and savagery;
4. Do NOT blame me, SCOTUS, we do NOT have judicial review (non-justiciable), because we defer to the Political Question Doctrine of Congress' Plenary Power. Go back to Congress in order to fix whatever (treaty and/-or statute in question.

------

1824. Congress transferred the office of Indian affairs, now the Bureau of Indian Affairs, an Instrument of Cultural Oppression, from the Department of War, then to the Department of Defense, and ultimately to the newly founded Department of Interior.

1870. The U.S. had recognized the Indian tribes as semi-independent.

1871. The End of Treaties with Native Tribes, and the rise of the Doctrine of Plenary Power Trilogy Cases (Criminal Cases: Ex-parte Crow Dog; Kagama; Sandoval; and Land Case: Lone Wolf v. Hitcock). NOTE: The U.S. House of Representatives in Congress had little or nothing to say about Indian Affairs outside of appropriations. Treaties are negotiated between POTUS and an Indian tribe, and then ratified by the U.S. Senate, thereby leaving the House of Representatives NOT able to do anything.

The Indian Appropriations Act of 1871, an Instrument of Cultural Oppression, declared that Indigenous people were no longer considered members of "sovereign nations" and that the US government could no longer establish treaties with them. The Act effectively made Native Americans wards of the US government and paved the way for other laws that granted the federal government increased power over the land and lives of Indigenous peoples. Although it promised not to "invalidate or impair the obligation" of previous treaties, the act was the first step toward the elimination of Indigenous sovereignty, which was completed in 1898 with the Curtis Act, and the invalidation of previous treaty obligations, a power finally granted to Congress in 1903.

1817. The General Crimes Act, an Instrument of Cultural Oppression. Under 18 U.S.C. §1152 the general laws of the U.S. as to the punishment of crimes committed in any place within the sole and exclusive jurisdiction of the U.S., except the District of Columbia,... extend to the Indian country." The "laws" thus extended are those applicable within the Special Maritime and Territorial Jurisdiction of the U.S., as defined in 18 U.S.C. §7, popularly known as "federal enclave laws."

There are four exceptions to the coverage of §1152, three of them legislative and the fourth judicially created.

The second paragraph of 18 U.S.C. §1152 specifies the three legislative exceptions: This section shall not extend [1] to offenses committed by one Indian against the person or property of another Indian; nor [2] to any Indian committing any offense in the Indian country who has been punished by the local law of the tribe; or [3] to any case where, by treaty stipulations, the exclusive jurisdiction over such offenses is or may be secured to the Indian tribes respectively.

The fourth exception to the broad coverage of §1152 was created by

SCOTUS. Notwithstanding its literal terms, SCOTUS significantly narrowed the reach of 18 U.S.C. §1152 in *U.S. v. McBratney, 104, U.S. 621 (1882)*, holding that, absent treaty provisions to the contrary, the state has exclusive JX over a crime committed in the Indian country by a non-Indian against another non-Indian. Accord, *Draper v. U.S., 164 U.S. 240 (1896)*. Subsequent decisions have acknowledged the rule. *See, e.g., Williams v. U.S., 327 U.S. 711, 714 (1946); U.S. v. Antelope, 430 U.S. 641, 643 n. 2 (1977); U.S. v. Wheeler, 435, U.S. 313, 325 n. 21 (1978)*.

1872. The U.S. regulates Indian affairs through Statutes of Congress, Executive Orders of the POTUS, Rules and Regulations from the various departments under the Executive Branch, and common law of SCOTUS.

1878. The Indian police, an Instrument of Cultural Oppression. Congress approved the establishment of the federal Indian police and by 1890 nearly all reservations had them. The Indian police were created to enforce American law and the rules and regulations established by the Indian agent aka, tribal superintendent, or field agent.

1883. The Courts of Indian offenses, an Instrument of Cultural Oppression. The Department of Interior established the Rules of Indian courts. Code of Federal Regulations (Title 25, Chapter 1, Subchapter B, Part 11, Courts of Indian Offenses and Law and Order Code.

Indian courts were created to punish those who ran afoul of American law or the Indian agent/superintendent's rules. The Superintendent held great sway over the police, the courts, jobs, and rations, and sometimes accompanied police during arrests, appointing judges, or even acting as chief of police, and chief judge themselves.

The Indian courts established in this era are sometimes referred to as CFR courts, because their guidelines were found in Title 25, Code of Federal Regulations. Some tribal nations continue to operate CFR courts today, although they have much greater control over them now than they did during the allotment era.

Courts of Indian Offenses to prosecute tribal members had more to do with suppressing religious dances, and certain kinds of ceremonials rather than with keeping law and order; and prosecuted for practicing his or her traditional religion such as the Sun Dance aka Thirst Dance, Sweatlodge, engaging in traditional dancing, not dipping your sheep in oil, or cohabitating without being married under Western law. The U.S. sought to replace these ancient spiritual practices with Christianity. The court is one of various methods that the U.S. employs to try to restrict the cultural identity of American Indian tribes. Many, political, cultural, and spiritual leaders are imprisoned.

Many of the offenses handled by the police and the courts in the allotment era were common crimes, such as theft. However, as they were tools of the push toward civilization, both the police and the courts were often punished for those who violated the ethos of the "progress" the federal government sought to instill within reservations.

## 1883. *EX PARTE CROW DOG, 109 U.S. 556 (1883)*, THE FIRST FEDERAL INDIAN CRIMINAL CASE

- Facts: *Ex-parte Crow Dog*, Justice Stanley Matthews.
- Crow Dog, Rosebud Lakota murdered Brule Chief Spotted Tail. Following tradition, the family and tribes came together to decide on some means of restorative justice, meaning, "they would try to work out something for the best of the victim and family as well as the perpetrator." The worked out something that was acceptable to both, and had Crow Dog support Spotted Tail's family and offered provisions such as horses, blankets, and money.
- The federal government was NOT happy with the resolution. There was a lot of pressure to do something about this. They did NOT like that Crow Dog was NOT

punished by Western style law. U.S. Marshalls went into Rosebud and arrested Crow Dog, prosecuting him in a territorial court. He was found guilty of murder and sentenced to hang, but Crow Dog appealed his conviction (habeas corpus) with SCOTUS.

- Holding: SCOTUS held that Congress does NOT have the power to limit what Indian tribes can do, and unless Congress exercises that power, Indian tribes are permitted to govern however they wish.

- It tries them NOT by their peers, nor by the customs of their people, nor the law of their land, but by superiors of a different race, according to the law of a social state of which they have an imperfect conception and which is opposed to the traditions of their history, to the habits of their lives, to the strongest prejudices of their savage nature, one which measures the red man's revenge by the maxims of the white man's morality. The case in front of Justice Matthews, where the tribal court decided that Crow Dog should make apology to the next of kin of the man he killed and give them substantial property to show sincerity of both the apology and the promise of future behavior (NOT as restitution). Both Crow Dog and Spotted Tail (the victim) had many relatives and followers, and the tribal court was trying to avoid a Hatfield and McCoy style feud that could do untold harm to the peace of the reservation. That was, "the strongest prejudices of their savage nature." In contrast, "the white man's morality" decreed that Crow Dog should hang by the neck until dead, without regard to whether he posed a continuing threat to the peace of the community or the effect his death would have on the community.

- QUESTION: Which judgment reflects the "strongest prejudices of savage nature?"

TAKEAWAYS

Strong affirmation of tribal customary law and sovereignty, although in a very patronizing way. SCOTUS held that, unless authorized by Congress, federal courts had NO JX to try cases where the offense had already been tried by the tribal council. Wherein they overturned the federal court conviction of Brule Lakota sub chief Crow Dog who was convicted and sentenced to death for the murder of principal chief Spotted Tail on the Rosebud Sioux Indian Reservation in Dakota Territory. SCOTUS reasoned that the ability of the tribes to deal with such an offense was an attribute of tribal sovereignty that had NOT been specifically abrogated by an act of Congress.

WHATEVER HAS NOT BEEN TAKEN AWAY REMAINS

Ex-parte Crow Dog, was the impetus for early tribal court development, because SCOTUS recognized inherent right of Indian nations to resolve their own internal conflicts even for serious felonies. Tribal members are therefore subject only to their tribal laws, unless the U.S. expressly states otherwise.

Soon after, Congress passed the Indian Major Crimes Act, an Instrument of Cultural Oppression. And beginning in 1885, federal officials could arrest Indians who committed certain crimes in Indian country.

1885. The Indian Major Crimes Act.

An Instrument of Cultural Oppression. Congress responded to Ex-parte Crow Dog, by enactment of the Indian Major Crimes Act, 18 U.S.C. §1153; §3242 and granting federal courts JX over certain enumerated crimes, but not over minor offenses.

The FIRST STATUTE directly regulating the internal tribal affairs by imposing criminal liability on Indians committing major crimes against other Indians within Indian country.

Source of authority? Derived from the Indian Commerce Clause, See Art. 1, Sec. 8, Clause 3 of the U.S. Constitution.

## 1886. *UNITED STATES V. KAGAMA*

- Holding: SCOTUS upheld the constitutionality of the Indian Major Crimes Act. This Congressional Act gave the federal courts JX in certain cases of Indian-on-Indian crimes, even if the crimes were committed on an Indian reservation. The importance of the ruling in this case was that it tested the constitutionality of the Act and confirmed Congress' authority over Indian affairs. The plenary powers doctrine over Indian tribes, supposedly granted to the U.S. Congress by the Commerce Clause of the U.S. Constitution, was NOT necessary to supported by SCOTUS in this decision, instead, SCOTUS found the power in the tribe's status as dependent domestic nations. This allowed Congress to pass the Dawes Act the following year.

TAKEAWAYS

This case has been criticized by legal scholars as drawing on powers that are NOT granted to Congress by the Constitution. It remains good law, despite that criticism. SCOTUS has sustained the constitutionality of the "Indian" Major Crimes Act. SCOTUS canvassed the enumerated powers in the Constitution, finding each in turn insufficient. SCOTUS nevertheless upheld the MCA on two theories: [1] That only the U.S., as opposed to the states, is sovereign over the entire territory of the U.S.; and [2] That the U.S.'s role as the guardian of Indians, Indian tribes, and their property justifies any legislation enacted in this role of guardian. Therefore, according to SCOTUS, Congress has absolute power over Indian tribes.

1776-1887 The U.S. seized over 1.5 billion acres from America's Indigenous people by treaties and Executive orders.

MOST DETRIMENTAL FEDERAL ACT

1887. The Dawes Act or the General Allotment Act. Authorized

POTUS to survey American Indian tribal land and divide it into allotments for individual Indians. Those who accepted allotments and live separately from the tribe would be granted U.S. citizenship. Sometimes it was up to twenty-five years, but could have been sooner, and always at the discretion of the Indian agent.

See Lone Wolf v. Hitchcock, 187 U.S. 553 (1903).

## 1888. *UNITED STATES V. CLAPOX, 35 F. 575 AT 577 (D. OR. 1888)*

- Facts: Minnie a member of the Umatilla tribal nation, was jailed for adultery. Although NOT a violation of federal or tribal law. Minnie was nonetheless charged under rules created by the Bureau of Indian Affairs in their efforts to "civilize" the Umatilla. Clapox and a number of other tribal members broke Minnie out of the jail. After being captured, Clapox and the others essentially argued that Minnie had been unlawfully held, that the federal government did NOT have the authority to establish Indian courts, and that since Minnie was unlawfully held, the rescuers did NOT violate any law by rescuing her.

- Holding: CFR Courts were Assimilative and were described as: These "courts of Indian offenses" are NOT the constitutional courts provided for in Section 1, Article 3, of the U.S. Constitution, which Congress only has the power to "ordain and establish," but mere educational and disciplinary instrumentalities, by which the government of the U.S. is endeavoring to improve and elevate the condition of these dependent tribes to whom it sustains the relation of guardian. In fact, the reservation itself is in the nature of a school, and the Indians are gathered there, under the charge of an agent, for the purpose of acquiring the habits, ideas, and aspirations which distinguish the civilized from the uncivilized man.

———

TAKEAWAYS

CFR courts still exist today, primarily in OK; but can also be found in Fort Washakie, WY; and on the Ute Mountain Ute Reservation.

Although the old U.S. v. Clapox decision had upheld the validity of the courts, the BIA had always avoided litigation involving Indians who had become citizens, now it would be difficult to avoid such a test without giving up the courts entirely.

1896. Tribal powers are NOT limited by the U.S. Constitution. There is nothing in the Constitution that requires Indian tribes to conform their powers of self-government to its provisions. Tribal governments, thus may enact laws that would violate the U.S. Constitution, if those same laws had been enacted by the federal, or state governments.

## TALTON V. MAYES, 163 U.S. 376 (1896)

- Facts: After the Cherokees were relocated to Oklahoma, Bob Talton, Cherokee, was arrested for murdering another Cherokee man on the reservation. Talton was charged, and convicted of the murder of a fellow Cherokee. He was sentenced to death by hanging after a trial that took place between May and December 1892. The appellant appealed the decision in federal court on the basis that the tribal court had denied his constitutional rights, a violation of his rights by being in contradiction to the law. The U.S. Constitution and, by the end of his trial, the Cherokee laws, demanded more than the five Grand Jury members furnished by the Cherokee courts.
- Issue: The question was, did he, or any Indian have constitutional rights under tribal law?
- Holding: SCOTUS held that the individual rights protections, which limit the federal government through the 5$^{TH}$ Amendment, and later state governments through the 14$^{TH}$ Amendment, do NOT apply to tribal governments. If reaffirmed earlier decisions, such as the *Cherokee Nation v.*

*Georgia* case which held that Indian tribes have a status as "domestic dependent nations," the sovereignty of which is independent of the federal government.

TAKEAWAYS

Consistent with *Worcester*, tribal law was upheld and Talton was found guilty under tribal law. Upholding the doctrine of Indian tribal sovereignty. Rigorously applies the Marshall Model: Whatever has NOT been taken away remains. The Marshall Model trumps tribal sovereignty, until Congress changes it. Q. Are Indian tribes subject to the U.S. Constitution? A. Nothing in the Cherokee/U.S. Treaty, NO statute, and in the absence of Congress, SCOTUS will NOT apply the Bill of Rights. At the time, the Bill of Rights did NOT apply to the States either, until incorporation by the 14$^{TH}$ Amendment. Parallelism to the states and tribes. Until Congress changes the situation, Indian tribes can do whatever they want to their own members, as long as they have JX over them.

Tribal sovereignty under the Marshall Model, is outside of the U.S. Constitution, and tribes are NOT subject to the restraints of the U.S. Constitution. Indian tribal governments are NOT subject to the U.S. Constitution, (*see Talton*, and *see Wheeler*).

1903. The Allotment Era, (allotment treaties), and SCOTUS' deference for Congressional plenary power in Indian affairs reached its peak in the case of *Lone Wolf v. Hitchcock, 187 U.S. 553 (1903)*.

## *LONE WOLF V. HITCHCOCK, 187 U.S. 553 (1903)*

- Facts: By 1876, many tribes had already been relocated to reservations, and it was clear that treaties were repeatedly violated. When the Kiowa and Comanche were forced to sign a treaty, they agreed to the conditions, but wisely asked that they never have to relinquish any more land, unless three-quarters of the adult male tribal members agreed in a vote, taken by the federal government. The government agreed, and they signed the treaty of medicine creek. In 1871, Congress passed a law ending treaty making, but said existing treaties were NOT devalued or abrogated. When Congress moved to take more of the Kiowa and Comanche's land without an election, the tribes took the case to SCOTUS.

- Holding: SCOTUS ruled that just as a federal statute can amend and repeal an earlier statute, a federal statute can amend or repeal a treaty. Since the U.S. had always acted with authority over Indians, the power exists [in Congress] to abrogate the provisions of an Indian treaty. SCOTUS further stated that in the last sentence of the decision which read: "We must presume that Congress acted in perfectly good faith."
- To uphold the claim would be to adjudge that the indirect operation of the treaty was to materially limit and qualify the controlling authority of Congress in respect to the care and protection of the Indians, and to deprive Congress, in a possible emergency, when the necessity might be urgent for a partition and disposal of the tribal lands, of all power to act, if the assent of the Indians could NOT be obtained.


TAKEAWAYS

The claim Justice White feared upholding was that the government had NO authority to take Kiowa land without complying with the treaty that governed the relationship between the U.S., and the Kiowa Nation. The real emergency that placed Indians in dire danger was in the holding that Congress could abrogate Indian treaties without reference to the existing international law of treaty abrogation.

- Allotment, was NOT considered a taking.
- Money collected from the surplus lands, was taken as administrative fees.

- NO judicial review by SCOTUS. Indian affairs was considered like foreign affairs.

## THE INDIAN WATER RIGHTS

Indian water claims a very controversial body of law, and most often Indian treaties, are more likely to be superior to states, and private property owners.

## 1908. *WINTERS V. UNITED STATES*

- Facts: The Fort Belknap Indian Community (Gros Ventre, and Assiniboine) Reservation and the Milk River that runs along the highline in Montana are linked together by the treaties between the U.S. and the two tribes.
- Holding: SCOTUS held that a federal law setting aside lands for Indian exclusive use and occupancy, may also create Indian rights to water even in the absence of express language in the statute reserving those rights.

## THE INDIAN REORGANIZATION ERA

1924. The Forced Indian Citizenship Act, granted full U.S. citizenship to America's Indigenous peoples. Although Native people had lived on Turtle Island for generations, it was NOT until this Act was passed and unilaterally imposed upon Native people, were they granted the full birthright of U.S. citizenship. While the 14TH Amendment to the U.S. Constitution defined as citizens any person born in the U.S., the amendment had been interpreted to restrict the citizenship rights of most Native people. Some exceptions were given to WWI native veterans; and individual Indian allotees at the discretion of the Secretary of Interior.

·  ·  ·

1934. The Indian Reorganization Act of June 18, (1934), an Instrument of Cultural Oppression. The major goal was to reverse the traditional goal of assimilation of Indians into American society, and to strengthen, encourage, and perpetuate the tribes and their historic traditions and culture. The Act also restored to Indians the management of their assets, land, and mineral rights, and included provisions intended to create a sound economic foundation for the inhabitants of Indian reservations. To reverse assimilation policies and provide ways for American Indians to re-establish sovereignty and self-government, to reduce the losses of reservation lands, and establish ways for Indians to build economic self-sufficiency. The self-government provisions would automatically go into effect for a tribe, unless a clear majority of the eligible Indians voted it down. When approved, a tribe would adopt a variation of the model constitution drafted often times by BIA lawyers.

The United States Congress passed the Indian Reorganization Act (also known as the Wheeler-Howard Act) which provided for the federal recognition of tribal councils, and corporations upon the creation of such bodies, and the adoption of tribal constitutions, and/-or charters by a majority vote of tribal members.

NOTE: The IRA also created very weak Tribal courts, some with NO separation of executive government. Legislative and Executive are known as the Business Committee, some have NO Judicial Branch, and some are created by Resolution. The IRA authorized the legislative creation of tribal courts as well as the adoption of tribal law and order codes, with some subject to the review and approval of the U.S. Secretary of Interior.


1953. Public Law 83-280, an Instrument of Cultural Oppression.

Stand-alone statutes: KS, 18 USC 3243 (1940); ND, Devil's Lake/Spirit Lake reservation (1946); IA (1948); NY, 25 USC 232 (1949).


From 1953-63, the federal policy was to terminate the federal trust responsibility and transfer JX (primarily criminal JX) to the states, whereby states may assume JX (except for wildlife offenses) over reservation Indians. There are two types of PL-280 jurisdictional transfers: [1] mandatory PL-280; and [2] optional PL-280.

Mandatory PL-280 refers to the JXs listed at 18 U.S.C. §1162(a). States included are AK, CA, MN (except Red Lake reservation), NE, OR (except Warm Springs reservation), and WI.

Optional PL-280, between 1953-68, the state has JX over whatever types of offenses that it has accepted under state law.

1956. The Indian Relocation Act, the other IRA, an Instrument of Cultural Oppression. Aka the Adult Vocational Training Program, was intended to encourage Native Americans in the U.S. to leave Indian reservations, acquire vocational skills, and assimilate into the general population. Part of the Indian termination policy of that era.

Retained inherent adjudicatory and regulatory civil JX ("clear as mud"). *Williams v. Lee (1959); and Montana v. U.S. (1981).*

## 1959. *WILLIAMS V. LEE, 358 U.S. 217, 223 (1959)*

"The Infringement Test."

- Facts: Lee, a non-Indian trader on the Navajo Reservation, brought a civil suit against Williams, a Navajo man, to retrieve some items that the Navajo man had purchased on credit from Lee's Ganado Trading Post. Lee brought his lawsuit in AZ court, but Williams challenged the suit, claiming that only tribal court had JX over the dispute.
- Issue: Whether state law can be applied on reservation lands absent Public Law 280 or any other treaty or statute. Does a state law infringe on the rights of reservation Indians to make their own laws and be ruled by them? If yes, then the state law is invalid in Indian country. If no, then state law is applicable in Indian country.

- Holding: Williams was on the reservation and the transaction with an Indian took place there. The cases in this Court have consistently guarded the authority of Indian governments over their reservations. Congress recognized the authority in the Navajos in the Treaty of 1868, and has done so ever since. If this power is to be taken away from them, it is for Congress to do it.

TAKEAWAYS

Whatever has NOT been taken away, remains.

## THE SELF-DETERMINATION ERA

1962 – Present.

Revitalization of tribal entities improvement of conditions on reservations, passage of the ICRA.

In this era of self-determination, tribal courts are continuing to rely on Indigenous systems, values, and ideas and are incorporating and improving on aspects of Western legal systems so that they can competently address the full range of cases under their JX, from disagreements between families to multimillion-dollar disputes between tribal entities and non-Native litigants.

The "Indian Bill of Rights," an Instrument of Cultural Oppression. Retained Diminished Dependent Tribal Sovereignty.

1968. The Indian Civil Rights Act, the SECOND STATUTE directly regulating the internal tribal affairs by imposing an Indian Bill of Rights. The primary statutory tool for federal regulation of tribal court criminal procedure. Congress expressly and intentionally codified the unsettled tension between individual rights and group rights in tribal communities. The ICRA contains several restrictions on Indian tribal governments. The Act extends many provisions in the Bill of Rights to individuals in their dealings with tribal governments. The tribal law of individual rights is entirely foreign, imposed from on high by the U.S. government, the colonizer, the trustee. But judicial interpretation of the Act supports tribal autonomy, even in the face of claim deprivations of important individual rights. The Act also contained provisions requiring the U.S. Secretary of Interior to revise the *Handbook of Federal Indian law*, by Felix S. Cohen; a model law and order code for tribal governments; and rules regarding the appointment of legal counsel by tribes. The ICRA also set out procedures that tribes must extend to criminal defendants in tribal courts, caps sentencing authority and fines imposed, and defines criminal JX.

## WHAT ARE SOME EXAMPLES OF WHAT IS INSIDE THE ICRA

- Free Speech
- Equal Protection
- Exercise of Religion
- Self-incrimination
- Takings clause
- Cruel and unusual punishment
- Double jeopardy
- Search and seizure
- Speedy public trial
- Jury
- Excessive bail
- Free press
- Attainder
- Ex-post facto
- Probable cause

## WHAT IS NOT INSIDE THE ICRA

- Article I, Clause I, NO right respecting the establishment of religion
- Article II, NO right to bear arms
- Article III, NO quartering of soldiers

- NO republic form of government
- NO privilege and immunity
- NO civil jury trial
- NO free public defender, unless the participating tribe adopts the 2010 TLOA provisions and/-or the 2013, or 2022 VAWA provisions.

1975. The Indian Self-Determination and Education Assistance Act (1975). The beginning of tribal self-determination.

Congress appropriates money for every Indian tribe. The tribe can then go to the Department of Interior, usually the Bureau of Indian Affairs, or the Department of Health and Human Services, usually the Indian Health Service and negotiate an annual funding agreement. This is an opt-in Act for tribes to participate. NOTE: Tribes became federal government contractors for the provision of services to themselves. Tribes can pick and choose from the menu which line-items out of every government service that the BIA, or IHS used to provide.

The Act authorized the U.S. Secretary of Interior, Secretary of Health, Education, and Welfare, and some other government agencies to enter into contracts with, and make grants directly to, federally recognized Indian tribes. The tribes would have authority for how they administered the funds, which gave them greater control over their welfare. The Act made self-determination the focus of government action. The Act reversed a thirty-year effort by the federal government under its preceding termination policy to sever Treaty relationships with and obligations to Indian tribes.

## IMPLICIT DIVESTITURE DEPENDENT TRIBAL SOVEREIGNTY

The 1978 Trilogy Cases.

## *OLIPHANT V. SUQUAMISH INDIAN TRIBE (1978)*, (MAJORITY 6-2), JUSTICE WILLIAM REHNQUIST, CASE REGARDING CRIMINAL JURISDICTION OF TRIBAL COURTS OVER NON-INDIANS, [AN INSTRUMENT OF CULTURAL OPPRESSION]

- Facts: On a small reservation in Washington State on Bainbridge Island, there were three-thousand (3,000) non-Indian residents and only fifty (50) Indian residents. This where Mark Oliphant, a white man, got drunk at the Chief Sealth, Suquamish Indian Days annual pow-wow. The tribal police told him to leave, and Oliphant punched the tribal officer, then got in his car and recklessly drove away, nearly running people over. Only by ramming his car off the road were the tribal police able to stop him. Oliphant was prosecuted and imprisoned for violating tribal laws. Oliphant appealed to SCOTUS, arguing that he was white and that the tribe did NOT have JX over him, that they can only exercise their authority over tribal members.
- The tribe argued that Congress had never limited tribal JX to Indians, and that *Worcester* Rule applied (state law shall have NO force in Indian country).
- Issue: Whether Indian tribes can prosecute non-Indians who commit crimes against an Indian (in this case a tribal police officer employed by the tribe), in Indian country?
- Holding: Indian tribes do NOT have criminal JX to prosecute non-Indian U.S. citizens in Indian country, absent U.S. consent.
- NOTE: Had previous principles been upheld, the tribe should have won. SCOTUS wanted the tribe to lose, so SCOTUS had to come up with a new principle. SCOTUS came up with a new doctrine that kept Indian tribes from exercising powers terminated by Congress as well as "those inconsistent with their status."
- NOTE: Now SCOTUS can just say, "Indians should NOT have that power. It is inconsistent to us." This is a perfect example of racism. There is NO way to explain this case, except for racism, if SCOTUS had followed the 175-year-old

principles of law. NOTE: Most influential SCOTUS decision in the modern-day era. Marks a shift in jurisprudence towards Indian nations, and continues to happen to present day, as of this writing 2022.

- Tribal nations do NOT have the inherent authority to criminally prosecute non-Indians through the Implicit Divestiture Doctrine because of their domestic dependent status. The Balancing Test – The *McBratney* Rule (non-Indian versus non-India in Indian country); the *Williams v. Lee* Test is NOT met, the tribal self-government is NOT met. SCOTUS is going to create another CATEGORICAL RULE. Indian tribes do NOT have criminal JX over non-Indian U.S. citizens, absent Congressional consent. NOTE: Worst case scenario of facts to argue for tribal JX. Tribal Appellate court; U.S. District court; and the 9[TH] Circuit court of appeals all upheld tribal JX. SCOTUS overturned. Tribe argues inherent tribal sovereignty, presumably criminal JX over all on Indian lands. Justice Rehnquist describes the Indian tribal courts without law nor by formal judicial processes.
- The opinion starts out with a discussion of the Port Madison Reservation of the Suquamish Indian Tribe. An allotted reservation. FOOTNOTE 1 – Demographic Footnote. Majority consists of non-Indian 63% (2,928) of land owned by non-Indians; versus 37% only about fifty (50) members of the tribe live on the reservation. Out of the 2978 people on the reservation, only fifty (50) are truly represented and can sit on the tribal council or tribal juries, and they exercise JX. Probably a full-time jury pool of only about fifteen (15) people. NO right for non-Indians to sit on the jury.
- Bias question: Where would you move this case to? Answer: Nowhere. Only fifty (50) truly have a right to representation. Daniel Belgarde and Mark Oliphant.
- NOTE: Oliphant was a long-time resident of the reservation. Attorneys for the tribe do NOT base their argument on a Treaty or Statute, but base their argument upon the Marshall Model: Whatever has NOT been taken away, remains.

- Rehnquist says that the exercise of criminal JX by tribal courts is a new-phenomena and when it has been addressed is has been concluded that JX did NOT exist.

## HISTORICAL OVERVIEW

FIRST AUTHORITY:

Whether or NOT Indians have JX, Rehnquist cites to an 1834 commissioner of Indian affairs under President Jackson, who carried out genocide acts against Indians, during the removal era.

SECOND AUTHORITY:

Preference of formal systems versus non-formal systems. And in the earliest treaties it was assumed that Indian tribes lack JX. Look at the removal treaty of the Choctaw, guaranteed Indian tribe JX of persons and properties within their limits, and Congress may grant to the Choctaw JX over Whitemen. NOTE: Rehnquist takes to be the assumption of NO JX without express Congressional delegation.

THIRD AUTHORITY:

Ex-parte Kenyon, written by Judge Parker. NO judge has been overturned more in U.S. history than Judge Parker. Court considered Indian JX and concluded against.

FOURTH AUTHORITY:

1970 Opinion of the Solicitor of the Interior that Indian tribes have NO JX which was withdrawn.

Footnote 11. Opinion of the Solicitor was withdrawn in 1974, but has NOT been replaced.

NOTE: Rehnquist does NOT have a case yet. Still looking for precedent. If you want to find bad documents against Indians, go back to the Removal Era. He has to reach back 150 years to find authority to cite.

. . .

FIFTH AUTHORITY:

1834 Congress (during the removal era) first considered JX and drafted legislation that was never passed that would have denied Indian tribes the right to have criminal JX over Whitemen.

Footnote 13. Citing a Western Territory Bill, that was never passed into law.


SIXTH AUTHORITY:

1960 Senate Report, during the termination era, assumed that Indian tribes did NOT have JX over non-Indians.

1960, the height of the termination era. That body of federal Indian law expressly assumed that Indian tribes lacked criminal JX over non-Indians.

NOTE: Rehnquist concluded that it is "an unspoken assumption," that Congress has a commonly shared assumption of Congress, Executive branch, and the Courts that Indians do NOT have JX over non-Indians.

NOTE: Indian law must be read in light of the common assumptions of the day of those that drafted them. You are supposed to look at the mindset of those that make Indian policy to answer ambiguity and because they would never have conceded to JX over non-Indians that becomes part of the interpretive matrix.

NOTE: Unspoken assumption that Indian tribes lacked criminal JX over non-Indians.


RULE: While Congress never expressly forbade Indian tribes to impose criminal penalties on non-Indians, we now make express our implicit conclusion of nearly a century ago that Congress consistently believed this to be the necessary result of its repeated legislative actions.

. . .

NOTE: INDIAN LAW draws principally upon the treaties drawn and executed by the Executive branch and legislation passed by Congress. These instruments, which beyond their actual text form the backdrop for the intricate web of judicially made Indian law, can NOT be interpreted in isolation, but must be read in light of the common notions of the day and the assumptions of those who drafted them.

## *WORCESTER V. GEORGIA, (1832)*

By acknowledging their dependence upon the U.S., Indians "in all probability" assumed that the U.S. would arrest and try non-Indian intruders. NOTE: But, Treaties must be construed liberally in favor of the Indians.

Footnote 17. Do NOT need to apply the canons of construction, statutory provisions NOT clear on their face may be clear form surrounding circumstances and legislative history. NOTE: Rehnquist says that Congress never took away the right to have JX over the non-Indians because Indian tribes NEVER HAD SUCH JX absent Congressional delegation (citing the theory of the Doctrine of Discovery) *see Johnson v. McIntosh (1823); and also see Cherokee Nation v. Georgia (1831).*

NOTE: Taking Cohen head on: Whatever has NOT been taken away, remains. NOT exactly!

This is back to Calvin's case: Upon incorporation under the Doctrine of Discovery, at that moment, their criminal JX was wiped out as a necessary implication of their Indian tribes' dependent status.

Used to think there were two (2) limitations upon Indian tribal sovereignty:

[1] The right to sell land to whoever they please; and

[2] The right to make Treaties with other nations.

But there is another principle there and the Doctrine of Discovery must be a dynamic principle that protects the sovereign interests of the U.S. and limits Indian sovereignty wherever the interest are in conflict.

NOTE: Protection of territory has always been central to the sovereign interest of the U.S., so that is the test:

DOES THE EXERCISE OF TRIBAL POWERS SOMEHOW EFFECT THE SOVEREIGN INTERESTS OF THE UNITED STATES?

By submitting to the overriding sovereignty of the U.S., Indian tribes give up their power to try non-Indians except as provided by and acceptable to Congress.

NOTE: This is an invitation to Congress to use a delegation model to delegate to Indian tribes JX.

THIS IS A MONUMENTAL POWER SHIFT IN POLICY.

Supposed to be within the purview of Congress and NOT within the Court.

## EX-PARTE CROW DOG, (1883)

The inverse of this case where tribal courts have exclusive JX over Indian on Indian crime, given the unique nature of Indian tribes. Using that same logic, non-Indians should NOT be subject to those Indian courts. Rehnquist said that Indians should NOT be tried in white courts, therefore whites should NOT be tried in Indian courts, citing *Ex-parte Crow Dog (1883)* in which Congress followed up by enacting the Indian Major Crimes Act (1885). NOTE: But, Crow Dog's conduct was killing an Indian on Indian land, and he was charged and convicted by tribal law, and then charged and convicted to hang by a federal court; and Oliphant's conduct assaulting a tribal police officer was not on state land, but on Indian land.

The Doctrine of Discovery protects unwarranted intrusions on the JX of the U.S. by Indian tribes.

Instead of whatever has NOT been taken away remains.

NOW IT IS:

WHATEVER INTERFERES WITH THE SOVEREIGN OF THE UNITED STATES HAS BEEN TAKEN AWAY BY OPERATION OF THE DOCTRINE OF DISCOVERY, UNLESS CONGRESS THROUGH DELEGATION, GIVES IT BACK TO YOU ("Indian tribes").

The problem with delegation is that Indian sovereignty has always been viewed as pre-Constitutional. The Analysis is different for an exercise of tribal power that arises after the Constitution. Rehnquist is saying that Indian JX over non-Indians was lost at Discovery, and any attempt by Congress to give it back is limited by the Bill of Rights.

NOTE: The question is this: If tribal JX evaporates at the point of contact, and the Bill of Rights constrains Congress, then Congress can only delegate in a way that is consistent with Due Process and the Bill of Rights.

OLIPHANT seems to restrict Congressional power in Indian affairs, and would seem to limit delegations by Congress.

After OLIPHANT, if Congress attempts to delegate, then they would have to give Equal Protection like GIDEON v. WAINRIGHT, (1963) (the Sixth Amendment's guarantee of a right to assistance of counsel applies to criminal defendants in state court by way of the Fourteenth Amendment).

Dissent: Justice Thurgood Marshall dissented, saying he believes that the right to punish all individuals who commit crimes against tribal law with the reservation is a necessary aspect of tribes' sovereignty. In his dissent, Justice Marshall states: "I agree with the court below that the 'power to preserve order on the reservation...is a sine qua non of the sovereignty that the Suquamish originally possessed.' Oliphant v. Schlie, 544 F.2d 1007, 1009 (CA9 1976). In the absence of affirmative withdrawal by Treaty or statute, I am of the view that Indian tribes enjoy, as a necessary aspect of their retained sovereignty, the right to try and punish all persons who commit offenses against tribal law within the reservation. Accordingly, I dissent." Chief Justice Warren E. Burger joined the dissenting opinion.


TAKEAWAYS
Key Principles from OLIPHANT.
How does the Court do it?
See Johnson v. McIntosh; and the Rogers cases.
SCOTUS diverges from what we thought was the Marshall Model. Felix Cohen: Whatever has NOT been taken away remains. SCOTUS does NOT apply the canons of construction, but now looks at incorporating the "Assumption of the Day."

[1] NO Treaties with Indian tribes seeking to engage in foreign relations; and

[2] NO alienate their Indian lands to non-Indians without federal consent.

After OLIPHANT, SCOTUS adds [3] By submitting to the overriding sovereignty of the United States, Indian tribes give up their power to try non-Indians except as provided by, and acceptable to the United States Congress.

CITING SOME OF THE VERY WORDS FROM CROW DOG, JUSTICE REHNQUIST WROTE FOR THE COURT:

Until the middle of this century, few Indian tribes maintained any semblance of a formal court system. Offenses by one Indian against another were usually handled by social and religious pressure, and NOT by formal judicial processes; emphasis was on restitution, rather than on punishment. While it's refreshing that 'the white man's morality" in this case recognized that there is more to justice than punishment, Rehnquist deployed these remarks as a part of a "history" made up to justify taking away tribal court JX over non-Indians who commit crimes on Indian land.

NOTE: 2013 – Republicans in the las Congress gave us a replay of this battle when they held up reauthorizing the Violence Against Women Act over allowing tribal courts to try non-Indian men who come on Indian country and abuse Indian women. NOTE: That was NOT their only objection to VAWA, but it was the one that made the most noise.

NOTE: Tribal courts would still have the power to enforce criminal contempt, power to enforce subpoenas, and power to exclude unwanted persons from the reservation (a Treaty provision) against disruptive non-Indians, and would therefore NOT be inconsistent with the status of a tribe as a dependent sovereign.

## UNITED STATES V. WHEELER, 435 U.S. 313 (1978), 9-0

- Facts: Navajo Indian defendant pled guilty in Navajo Tribal

Court to disorderly conduct and contributing to the delinquency of a minor. A year after the tribal prosecution, the defendant was indicted in federal court for rape arising out of the same incident.
- Issue: The controlling question is the source of an Indian tribe's power to punish tribal offenders, *i.e.,* whether it is a part of inherent tribal sovereignty, or an aspect of the sovereignty of the federal government that has been delegated to the tribes by Congress?

The U.S. Attorney brings this case, because of the issue of FORUM SHOPPING. Forum shopping is defined as the practice by some litigants to get their legal case heard in the court though most likely to provide a favorable judgment. It was the federal government which argued under the "dual sovereignty" principle of *Bartkus v. Illinois, 359 U.S. 121 (1959)* prosecutions by separate sovereigns are NOT "for the same offense," and therefore do NOT violate Double Jeopardy. Double jeopardy is defined as a procedural defense that forbids a defendant form being tried again on the same, or similar charges following a legitimate acquittal or conviction. Thus, although a prosecution by a city does bar prosecution by the state, because the city is a subdivision of the state; a prosecution by a state does NOT bar prosecution by the federal government, because both are separate sovereigns.

Whether the Double Jeopardy Clause of the Fifth Amendment bars the prosecution of an Indian in federal district court under the Major Crimes Act, when he has previously been convicted in a tribal court of a lesser included offense arising out of the same incident?

The Court of Appeals had held that this principle did NOT apply in this case, because the tribes are NOT sovereign themselves, but rather they derive their power to punish crimes from the federal government.

- Holding: Answer to the Issue is NO. SCOTUS held that Indian tribes "remains 'a separate people, with the power of regulating their internal and social relations.'" *Citing U.S. v. Kagama, and Cherokee Nation v. Georgia.*

SCOTUS further stated, "[I]t is evident that the sovereign power to punish tribal offenders has never been given up by the Navajo Tribe and that tribal exercise of that power today is therefore the continue exercise of retained tribal sovereignty."

In sum, the power to punish offenses against tribal law committed by tribal members, which was part of the Navajo's primeval sovereignty, has never been take away from them, either explicitly, or implicitly, and is attributable in NO way to any delegation to them of federal authority. If follows that when the Navajo Tribe exercises this power, it does so as part of its retained sovereignty and NOT as an arm of the federal government. Since tribal and federal prosecutions are brought by separate sovereigns, they are NOT "for the same offense," and the Double Jeopardy Clause thus does NOT bar one when the other has occurred. Put another way, the Double Jeopardy Clause of the U.S. Constitution does NOT bar the federal prosecution.


TAKEAWAYS

Explicit analogy to the pre-sovereign status like states; and Dual Sovereignty Doctrine, treating tribes like states.

QUESTION: What happens between *Talton v. Mayes*, and *U.S. v. Wheeler*, that separates tribes from states? ANSWER: States do become subject to the Bill of Rights, by incorporation through the 14[TH] Amendment, while tribes are NOT. Congress attempts to intervene to correct or remedy this situation by passing the ICRA. But even the ICRA fails to bring tribes into the same constitutional orbit as states.

NOTE: Tribal nations have to be careful about their particular authority, and if you step out of bounds you may get hurt. In sum, Indian tribes still possess those aspects of sovereignty NOT withdrawn by Treaty or Statute, or by Implication as a Necessary Result of their Dependent Status, *see Oliphant v. Suquamish Tribe*.

QUESTION: What if SCOTUS when the other way, and ruled that tribal courts are an extension of the federal courts, where would you advise your client to go?

ANSWER: Go to the court that would limit your client's punishment.

This case was an affirmation of tribal sovereignty; and the federal government to enforce any crimes over the ICRA limitations imposed upon the tribes of six (6) months and/-or five ($500) hundred dollars or both.

NOTE: SCOTUS noted that the issue was whether an Indian tribe had the inherent sovereignty to punish tribal members for offenses. SCOTUS held that Congress has plenary power to limit or abolish tribal power, but tribal power does NOT derive from Congress. (*See U.S. v. Rogers*). Tribal power drives from the tribe's sovereignty, and tribes exercise this power in the courts. SCOTUS observed that unless the power was withdrawn by Treaty or Statute, the tribe retained that authority. Since the Navajo Nation had never given up that authority, and Congress had NOT withdrawn it by Statute, the tribe could punish its members for violation of tribal law. Since the authority was separate from federal authority, the tribe was acting as an independent sovereign. The Double Jeopardy Clause does NOT prohibit prosecution by two separate sovereigns.

NOTE: SCOTUS also decided that tribal courts are the proper forum for civil disputes arising on tribal land [*see Williams v. Lee, 358 U.S. 217, 223 (1958)*]; and internal affairs, including internal disputes, are exclusively within JX of tribal government [*see Santa Clara Pueblo v. Martinez, 436 U.S. 49, 65-66 (1978)*]; and tribal remedies must be exhausted before a federal review can occur in cases regarding federal and diversity questions [*see Iowa Mut. Co. v. LaPlante, 480 U.S. 9, 15-16 (1987)*].

1968-78. For ten years, the federal courts took JX over claims of civil rights violations involving the application of the ICRA by tribal governments. Such cases included but were NOT limited to: tribal elections; reapportionment of voting districts; employee rights; criminal and civil proceedings; membership; police activities; and tribal council meetings.

## SANTA CLARA PUEBLO V. MARTINEZ 439, U.S. 49 (1978)

- Facts: Involved a request to stop denying tribal membership to those children born to female (NOT male) tribal members who married outside of the tribe. Julie Martinez pleaded that the discrimination against her child was solely based on sex, which violated the ICRA.
- Holding: SCOTUS decided that the federal remedy provided for in the ICRA was only a Habeas Corpus.

TAKEAWAYS

This decision ultimately strengthened tribal-self determination by further providing that generally, the federal government played NO enforcement role over the tribal governments.

NOTE: Look to a specific tribe's constitution that has the language, "subject to the approval of the U.S. Secretary of the Interior, governing future membership and the adoption of the new members."

The Indian Child Welfare Act (1978), 25 U.S.C. 1901-1963, P.L. 95-608, 92 Stat. 3069. The Act established federal rules to ensure that Indian children removed from their homes are place with Indian families whenever possible to preserve cultural values.

## MISSISSIPPI CHOCTAW INDIANS V. HOLYFIELD, 109 S.CT. 1597, 490 U.S. 30, 42-54, 104 L.ED.2D 29 (1989), JUSTICE WILLIAM BRENNAN

- Facts: The birth parents, both citizens of the Mississippi Band of Choctaw Indians were pregnant with twins and decided to give both up for adoption to a non-Indian couple who lived off the reservation. They moved near the adoptive non-Indian couple. After the twins were born, the birth parents went to state court and filed papers giving their consent to the adoption of their twins by the non-Indian couple.

- Holding: SCOTUS held the twins were "domiciled" on the tribe's reservation within the meaning of the ICWA's exclusive tribal JX provision, and the Chancery court was accordingly, without JX to enter the adoption decree.

TAKEAWAYS

The tribe did have JX over this matter, even if the birth and adoption happened off the reservation, and even if the birth parents temporarily moved off the reservation to evade the tribe's JX under ICWA.

The perceived implied limitations on the retained inherent regulatory (Legislative) and adjudicatory (Judicial) civil JX.

## *1981. U.S. V. MONTANA, 450 U.S. 544, 563-567 (1981)*, AN INSTRUMENT OF CULTURAL OPPRESSION

Balancing the Categorical Rules. SCOTUS then extended the *OLIPHANT* rule (Indian tribes do NOT have criminal JX over non-Indian, U.S. residents who commit crimes in Indian country.

- Facts: The case addressed the Crow Nation's ability to regulate hunting and fishing on tribal lands by a non-tribal member. The case considered several important issues concerning tribes' Treaty rights and sovereign governing authority on Indian reservations. The original dispute was over access to fishing on the Bighorn River within the exterior boundaries of the Crow Indian reservation in Montana. Plains hunting Indian tribe. There is clear evidence that the Crow fished on their rivers. This was an allotted Indian reservation. Along the rivers, there was the most heavily allotments. These allotments along the rivers, were deeded to the Railroads, and to the non-Indians. These non-Indian fee holders were being regulated by the Indian tribe to regulate non-Indian fishing and hunting on reservation land owned in fee [land inside the donut hole] by non-Indian non-members of the tribe. The Indian tribe is trying to regulate non-Indian fee land on the Indian reservation on the basis of their Treaty.

- Article II, Great Treaty language: "set apart for the absolute and undisturbed use and occupation of the Indians herein named and for such other friendly tribes or individual Indians as from time to time they may be willing, with the consent of the U.S. to admit amongst them…"

- Holding: SCOTUS held that the exercise of tribal power was beyond what is necessary to protect tribal self-government or to control internal relations is inconsistent with the dependent status of the tribes, and so canNOT survive without express Congressional delegation.

- General Rule: Indian tribes do NOT have civil JX over non-Indians on non-Indian fee lands within the reservation, except:

- [First exception]: Consensual Relationships (such as business contracts, marital contracts, leases); or

- [Second exception]: Political Integrity, the economic security, or the health, or welfare [Regulatory (Legislative) versus Adjudicatory (Judicial) is co-equal]. Here, regulation of hunting and fishing by non-members of the tribe on lands NO longer owned by the tribe bears NO clear relationship to tribal self-government or internal relations. Non-Indian hunters and fishermen on non-Indian fee land do NOT enter any agreements or dealings with the tribe so as to subject themselves to tribal civil JX. And nothing suggests that such non-Indian hunting and fishing so threaten the tribe's political or economic security as to justify tribal regulation.

TAKEAWAYS

How did SCOTUS get around this? See Footnote 9. It defies common sense to suppose that Congress intended that non-Indians purchasing allotted lands would become subject to tribal JX when an avowed purpose of the allotment policy was the ultimate destruction of tribal government.

SCOTUS does NOT apply the Canon of Construction, but now looks at incorporating the "Assumption of the Day."

*WHEELER* applies because of the Dual Sovereignty applied in *WHEELER*. *WHEELER* is a major part of the Modern Tribal Sovereignty, based upon the Marshall Mode.

SCOTUS takes a step back and applies *OLIPHANT*. There are limits of tribal sovereignty, based upon the Marshall Model. Delegation Issue. *WHEELER* Issue. All exercises of tribal power. NOTE: The principles were always there in *OLIPHANT* (which Justice Rehnquist just made up in that case) which now SCOTUS just assumes as always having been there.


FIRST AMENDMENT to the ICRA.

1986. Anti-Drug Abuse Act, Public Law 99-570. Tribal court sentencing limits and fines were raised. In 1986, this provision was amended as part of a federal drug and alcohol prevention Act to read: "in no event impose for conviction of any one offense any penalty or punishment great than imprisonment for a term of one year or a fine of $5000, or both." [see §1302(7)].


# INDIAN GAMING


## *CALIFORNIA V. CABAZON BAND OF MISSION INDIANS, 480 U.S. 202, 207-214 [1987], 6-3 JUSTICE WHITE*

- Facts: The Cabazon and Morongo Bands of Mission Indians, federally recognized Indian tribes, pursuant to an ordinance approved by the U.S. Secretary of Interior, conducts bingo

games on its reservation. Asserting that the bingo games on
the two reservations violated each of the states two
restrictions, California insisted that the tribes comply with
state law.

- Holding: Although state laws may be applied to tribal
  Indians on their reservations, if Congress has expressly
  consented, Congress has NOT done so here either by Pub. L.
  280 or by the Organized Crime Control Act of 1970.

1988. The Indian Gaming Regulatory Act, which recognizes Indian
gaming as a vehicle for achieving economic self-sufficiency on
reservations, and details the authority and role of tribal governments,
the federal government, and the states in Indian gaming.

## 1990. *DURO V. REINA 495 U.S. 676 (1990)*

- Facts: SCOTUS then extended the *OLIPHANT* rule and held
  that an Indian tribe lacked inherent sovereign powers to
  exercise criminal JX over non-member Indians is an
  "external" power, "inconsistent with the Indian tribe's
  dependent status" and thus capable of existing only by
  delegation from Congress, subject to the constraints of the
  U.S. Constitution.
- Issue: Whether Indian tribes can prosecute non-member
  Indians who commit crimes on their reservation?
- Holding: Indian tribes could NOT prosecute Indians who
  were members of other tribes for crimes committed by those
  non-member Indians on their reservation.

TAKEAWAYS

SCOTUS created a void in criminal JX. The federal courts had NO
criminal JX over non-member Indians who committed non-major
crimes in Indian country. The state did NOT have criminal JX over
non-member Indians absent P.L. 280. SCOTUS held that tribes could

NOT prosecute non-member Indians who committed crimes in Indian country.

## SECOND AMENDMENT to the ICRA

1991. *Duro*-Fix. Amending the ICRA in response to *Duro v. Reina*. The *Duro* decision held that tribal courts lacked criminal JX over non-member Indians. Congress overturned the Duro decision (the so-called Congressional Duro-fix) by adding language "and means the inherent power of Indian tribes, hereby recognized and affirmed, to exercise criminal JX over all Indians" to the definition of "powers of self-government. [see §1301(2)].

## TAKEAWAYS

This Congressional *Duro*-fix restored Indian tribe's inherent tribal court criminal JX over all Indians (members and non-members); and NOT as a delegation as SCOTUS stated in *OLIPHANT*.

## 1998. *KIOWA TRIBE OF OKLAHOMA V. MANUFACTURING TECHNOLOGIES INC.,* *523 U.S. 751 (1998),* THE DOCTRINE OF SOVEREIGN IMMUNITY

- Holding: SCOTUS reaffirmed the general rule that Indian tribes are immune from suit [1] absent consent, or [2] Congressional waiver.

## TAKEAWAYS

For SCOTUS, if tribal immunity is judge-made law, then perhaps SCOTUS can eliminate tribal immunity.

## 2004. *UNITED STATES V. LARA 541 U.S. 193 (2004)*, JUSTICE BREYER. THE MODERN PLENARY POWERS DOCTRINE

- Facts: Defendant Billy Jo Lara (a citizen of the Turtle Mountain Band of Chippewa) was charged for violating a banishment order and assaulting a BIA police officer under the Spirit Lake Tribal law, pled guilty, and was sentenced to ninety days incarceration. Federal prosecutor brought federal charges in federal district court for assaulting a federal police officer. Lara's attorney, Alex Richeirt, claimed double jeopardy against the federal charges.
- NOTE: We the U.S. Congress will define the meets and bounds of tribal sovereignty by calling SCOTUS' bluff on a delegation of authority to the Indian tribal sovereignty.

Q. How serious does delegation mean? Is that the only way that Indian tribes can get criminal JX over non-member Indians?

- Issue1: Whether Congress has the Constitutional power to relax restrictions that the political branches have, over time, placed on the exercise of a tribe's inherent legal authority?
- Rule1: Congress does possess this power pursuant to Article I, Section 8, Clause 3 – Indian Commerce Clause.
- Issue2: What is the source of the power to punish a non-member Indian offender, [a] inherent tribal sovereignty, or [b] delegated federal authority?
- Rule2: Pursuant to the ICRA, Congress has expressly stated by means of inherent power of Indian tribes, hereby recognized and affirmed, to exercise criminal JX over all Indians.
- Holding: Congress can restrict, or relax tribal sovereignty, and there is NO judicial review.
- SCOTUS ruled that double jeopardy did NOT apply to *LARA*, since the successive prosecutions were brought by

separate and distinct sovereign bodies. Affirming their own definition of tribal sovereignty traditional understanding of each tribe as a distinct political society, separated from others, capable of managing its own affairs and governing itself.

In 1885, Congress passed the Indian Major Crimes Act, divesting tribes of criminal JX in regard to several felony crimes.

In 1990, SCOTUS ruled in *Duro v. Reina* that an Indian tribe did NOT have the authority to try an Indian criminally who was NOT a member of that tribe.

In 1991, Congress amended the ICRA to recognize that Indian tribes have the inherent sovereignty and authority to try non-member Indians for crimes committed within the tribe's territorial JX.

Accepting as being outside the normal and pre-constitutional as necessary concomitants of national security.

We end up right back at *Calvin's case.*

The Sovereign can do what he wants and is NOT constrained by the Sovereign's Courts. We conclude that *DURO*, like several other cases, referred only to the need to obtain a Congressional statute that "delegate" power to the tribes. *See BOURLAND; and see also MONTANA.*

But in so stating, *DURO*, like the other cases, simply did NOT consider whether a statute, like the present one, could constitutionally achieve the same end by removing restrictions on the tribe's inherent authority. Consequently, we do NOT read any of these cases as holding that the Constitution forbids Congress to change "Judicially made" federal Indian law through this kind of Legislation. *See OLIPHANT.*

PROCEDURAL POSTURE

- Non-member assaults tribal police (BIA).
- He is prosecuted in tribal court, and he did NOT care.
- The U.S. prosecutes him, and his attorney, Alex Richeirt

asserts Double Jeopardy, under the Dual Sovereignty Exception. Billy Jo Lara had NOT objected.
- Issue of WHEELER'S dual sovereignty issue and its application to this case.
- Challenge to the U.S. Attorney's prosecution of Lara.

Q. We must decide whether Congress has the constitutional power to relax restrictions that the political branches have, over time, placed on the exercise of a tribe's inherent legal authority. ANSWER: YES.

- Very consistent with the *Calvin's case*.
- Rather, it enlarges the tribe's own "powers of self-government" to include "the inherent power of Indian tribes, hereby recognized and affirmed, to exercise criminal JX over all Indians."
- NOTE: Recognizing suspended (pre-constitutional powers) inherent to those tribes. Congress has the pre-Constitutional to adjust the meets and bounds of tribal sovereignty, NOT necessarily constrained by the Due Process and Equal Protection Clauses in the same way as other Constitutional decisions.

## *OLIPHANT, MONTANA,* AND THE MARSHALL MODEL

PLENARY POWER

Q. How can Congress have a pre-Constitutional right, when the Constitution created their rights?

A. Grants of pre-Constitutional power have always been there, it just has to be, [stop thinking about continuity, or making sense, it just has to be, it has to exist somewhere] *see Kagama*.

- Totally subject to the whim of Congress.
- Original intent reading of the Constitution.
- Original intent of the founder, whether or NOT the Indian

would be around, and even if they were going to be around, the federal government would help them assimilate.

- The Constitutionality.
- Limited sort of a change, NOT big and unusual. Consequently, we are NOT now faced with a question dealing with potential Constitutional limits on Congressional efforts to Legislate far more radical changes in tribal status [limiting infringement upon States].
- Justice Kennedy concurring:
- Here, contrary to this design, the National Government seeks to subject a citizen to the criminal JX of a third entity to be tried for conduct occurring wholly within the territorial borders of the Nation and one of the States. This is unprecedented.
- Justice Thomas, concurring:
- First, Congress rather than some other part of the Federal Government can regulate virtually every aspect of the tribes without rendering tribal sovereignty a nullity. *See Wheeler.*
- Deconstructs Indian law, and tribal sovereignty doctrine.

TAKEAWAYS

SCOTUS affirming their own definition of tribal sovereignty "traditional understanding" of each tribe as "a distinct political society, separated from others, capable of managing its own affairs and governing itself."

Commerce and Treaty Clauses and Structure of Constitution are basis for "Plenary and Exclusive" power of Congress.

Congress pursuant to Article I, Sec. 8, Cl. 3, passed the ICRA, and has "Expressly Stated," a requirement by SCOTUS to recognize Congress' Plenary Authority, "by means of inherent power of Indian tribes hereby recognized and affirmed, to exercise criminal JX over all Indians."

NOTE: SCOTUS had previously stated that Congress had to expressly state it, because according to SCOTUS Indian tribes do NOT inherently retain those rights under the Doctrine of Discovery, nor under the Domestic Dependent Nation "Trust" Doctrine.


## THIRD AMENDMENT to the ICRA

- 2010. Tribal Law and Order Act (TLOA).
- TLOA amends [1] Indian law enforcement reform Act; [2] Indian tribal justice Act; [3] Indian tribal justice technical and legal assistance Act of 2000; and [4] Omnibus crime control and safe streets Act of 1968.
- In order to impose these "enhanced sentencing" options, subject to greater than one-year imprisonment or a fine greater than $5,000, but not to exceed three years for any one offense; or impose on a person in a criminal proceeding a total penalty or punishment greater than imprisonment for a term of nine years; if certain conditions are met. Tribal courts shall provide certain additional, enumerated due process protections. These include the provision of effective defense counsel, and a licensed and law trained judge, making the tribal laws publicly available, maintain a record of the criminal proceeding,


## FOURTH AMENDMENT to the ICRA

- 2013. Violence Against Women Act (VAWA).
- Congress enacted VAWA, a limited change to the *Oliphant* rule. The Act authorizes concurrent tribal JX over certain non-Indians for domestic, or dating violence crimes, or violation of proactive orders dealing with related conduct, in order to utilize this "special domestic violence criminal JX," tribal courts shall have to provide certain enumerated due process protections. These include all of the TLOA of 2010 due process protections, [even if tribes do NOT impose the

enhanced sentencing options], as well as several additional due process protections including the right to an impartial jury.

- NOTE: A very narrow and partial OLIPHANT-fix. A participating tribe may exercise special domestic violence criminal JX over a defendant only if the defendant [1] resides in the Indian country of the participating tribe; [2] is employed in the Indian country of the participating tribe; or [3] is a spouse, intimate partner, or dating partner of [a] a member of the participating tribe; or [b] an Indian who resides in the Indian country of the participating tribe.
- NOTE: If neither of these apply, then there is NO criminal JX.

Person Personal JX

- Must have: [1] non-Indian perpetrator;
- AND [2] Indian victim.

Place Territorial JX

- Conduct must have occurred within Indian country defined, 18 U.S.C. §1151:
- [a] All land within reservation;
- [b] All dependent Indian communities;
- [c] All Indian allotments.

Law Subject Matter JX

- If charging non-Indian with Domestic Violence, then must have implemented VAWA 2013 requirements;
- If enhanced sentencing, then must have implemented TLOA 2010 requirements.

NOTE: VAWA 2013 was narrow for a reason, to create the strongest legal argument for the ability of Congress to enhance inherent tribal sovereignty, [the Acts covered are crimes in which tribes have a very significant interest in pursuing], and to get it passed through Congress by taking away as many objections as possible against its enactment. And it barely passed even with such a narrow and compelling scope.

Modifying the rule under *Talton v. Mayes*, requiring tribes to now provide for a minimum of six jurors; and addressing the jury pool found under Footnote 1 in *Oliphant*, requiring tribes to now provide the right to a trial by an impartial jury that is drawn from sources that reflect a fair cross section of the community, and do NOT systematically exclude any distinctive group in the community, including non-Indians.

NOTE: VAWA 2013 created a pilot project that authorized the Attorney General to grant an Indian tribe's request to begin exercising special domestic violence criminal JX earlier.

[1] Confederated Tribes of the Umatilla Indian Reservation; [2] Pascua Yaqui Tribe; [3] Tulalip Tribes. NOTE: The pilot project period ended March 7, 2015. Now any tribe that meets the federal statutory requirements can begin exercising jurisdiction. The Department of Justice approval is NO longer needed.

March 15, 2022. POTUS Biden signed into law the VAWA Reauthorization Act of 2022, which Congress passed as part of a larger consolidated appropriations Act, as part of the Omnibus funding bill. [See Division W. Pub. L. 117-103, 117TH Cong. (2022). Title VIII of the VAWA Reauthorization Act of 2022 builds on VAWA 2013's tribal JX provision (covering domestic violence, dating violence, and protection order violations), by incorporating additional categories of criminal conduct that can be prosecuted by tribes against non-Indians replacing the "special domestic violence criminal JX" authorized in the 2013 VAWA reauthorization with "special tribal criminal JX" over a broader range of "covered crimes," including assaulting against tribal justice personnel, crimes of violence against children, stalking, protection order violations, sexual violence, sex trafficking, and obstruction of justice, among others. [See Pub. L. 117-103, Title VIII, §804. VAWA 2022 also creates a pilot program for Indian tribes in Alaska to exercise special tribal criminal JX within Alaska native villages; provides formal authorization for the tribal access program (TAP); and reestablishes the U.S. bureau of prisons (BOP) tribal prisoner program first authorized as a pilot in the 2010 tribal law and order act (TLOA). The tribal provisions of VAWA 2022 are included in Title VIII of division W of the overall bill.

NOTE: With the passage of these amendments, tribes may now choose to exercise JX over additional crimes committed by non-Indians, provided they opt-in to the additional procedural protections. [See the ICRA as amended].

Native American Indian Tribes have retained inherent but some diminished tribal sovereignty over its own members when regulating its internal affairs; and have retained but severely diminished inherent tribal sovereignty over non-members when regulating its internal affairs stripped away over time by the U.S. federal government by Treaties, POTUS Executive Orders, regulations, Congressional Statutes, and SCOTUS common law decisions.

We are supposedly, currently in the Nation Building Era.

The importance of Judicial systems to Nation building. Having an effective tribal court system:

1. Advances tribal sovereignty
2. Supports economic growth
3. Empowers the Legislative and Executive Branches
4. Promotes peace and community health.

―――――

## NON-PUBLIC LAW 280

- Federal and Tribal concurrent jurisdiction
- NO federal delegation of jurisdiction to the states

Personal Jurisdiction (person)

- Federal Court - Federal definition [see U.S. v. Rogers, (1846); and U.S. v. Torres (1984)].
- State Court
- Tribal Court - Look to the specific Indian tribe's definition

[see tribal constitution, or statutes].

Subject Matter Jurisdiction (crime)
**Federal Court**

- ICCA
- GCA
- ACA
- Case Law

**State Court**

- Exclusive jurisdiction non-Indian versus non-Indian [*see McBratney (1881)*]; and
- Concurrent jurisdiction non-Indian versus Indian [*see Oklahoma v. Castro-Huerta (2022)*].

**Tribal Court**

- Look to the specific Indian tribe's constitution, statutes, case law, customs, and traditions.

Territorial Jurisdiction (place)

- Federal Court - Federal definition [see 18 U.S.C. §1151(a)(b)(c)].
- State Court - Federal definition [see 18 U.S.C. §1151(a)(b)(c)].
- Tribal Court - Federal definition [see 18 U.S.C. §1151(a)(b)(c)].

## PUBLIC LAW 280 (1953-1968-PRESENT)

State and Tribal concurrent jurisdiction

- Federal delegation of jurisdiction to the states, without federal funding.

- [Stand-alone statutes: North Dakota over Devil's Lake Reservation (1944); Iowa over the Meskwaki Settlement (1948); Kansas, and New York (1949)].
- Criminal Prohibitory; Civil Regulatory.

Personal Jurisdiction (person)

- Federal Court
- State Court - Look to the federal definition.
- Tribal Court - Look to the specific Indian tribe's definition [see tribal constitution, or statutes].

Subject Matter Jurisdiction (crime)

- Federal Court
- State Court - Look to the specific state constitution, statutes, and case law.
- Tribal Court - Look to the specific Indian tribe's constitution, statutes, case law, customs, and traditions.

Territorial Jurisdiction (place)

- Federal Court
- State Court - Federal definition [see 18 U.S.C. §1151(a)(b)(c)].
- Tribal Court - Federal definition [see 18 U.S.C. §1151(a)(b)(c)].

## NON-PUBLIC LAW 280 FEDERAL STATUTE 18 U.S.C. §1152

The Indian Country Crimes Act
General Crimes Act
aka Inter-Racial Crimes Act.
The victim IS relevant, for purposes of prosecuting the perpetrator.

The federal courts have exclusive jurisdiction if:

- [1] Indian versus non-Indian; and
- Concurrent jurisdiction with the states if:
- [2] non-Indian versus Indian [see Oklahoma v. Castro-Huerta (2022)].

These three exceptions shall NOT extend to the provisions if:

- [1] to offenses committed by one Indian against the person or property of another Indian; or
- [2] any Indian committing any offense in the Indian country who has been punished by the local law of the tribe; or
- [3] to any case where, by treaty stipulations, the exclusive jurisdiction over such offenses is or may be secured to the Indian tribes respectively.
- The fourth exception was created by SCOTUS, held that absent treaty provisions to the contrary, the state has exclusive jurisdiction over a crime committed in Indian country by a non-Indian against another non-Indian [*see U.S. v. McBratney (1882); and see Draper v. U.S. (1896)*].

## 18 U.S.C. §1153

- The Indian Major Crimes Act [applies only when the perpetrator (the criminal defendant) is an Indian].
- The victim is NOT relevant, for purposes of prosecuting the perpetrator.
- According to the language of the statute, the federal courts are supposed to have exclusive jurisdiction pursuant to 18 U.S.C. §3242. There are NO enumerated exceptions.
- SCOTUS has held that tribals courts may have concurrent jurisdiction with the federal courts, but tribes are limited on sentencing and/-or fines pursuant to the Indian Civil Rights Act of 1968 and its amendments.

## 18 U.S.C. §13

- The Assimilative Crimes Act.
- Allowing the borrowing of state law when there is NO applicable federal statute.
- The victim IS relevant, for purposes of prosecuting the perpetrator.
- If there is NO governing federal law, the federal government will look to the state crime in which the federal court sits, and assimilate that definition into federal court, even though the state law on its own would have NO force in Indian country.
- The Legislative History of the Act, indicated that Congress did NOT intend it to apply within Indian reservations.

What civil JX do Indian tribes have over non-Indians in Indian country? NOTE: SCOTUS uses non-Indian and non-member interchangeably.

Can Indian tribes regulate non-Indians on non-Indian fee lands within the reservation boundaries? The Montana Test. Indian tribes generally do NOT have civil JX over non-Indians, unless:

[1] The first exception to the Montana General Rule.

Covers activities of non-members who enter consensual relationships with the Indian tribes or its members, through commercial dealings, contracts, leases, or other arrangements.

Narrowing the first exception [see *Nevada v. Hicks, 533 U.S. 353 (2001)*]: Montana recognized an exception to this rule for tribal regulation of the activities of non-members who enter consensual relationships with the tribe or its members, through commercial dealings, contracts, leases, or other arraignments. Though the wardens in this case consensually obtained a warrant form the tribal court before searching respondent's home and yard, we do NOT think this qualifies as an "other arraignment" within the meaning of this passage. Read in context, an "other arraignment" is clearly another private consensual relationship, from which the official actions at issue in this case are far removed.

[2] The second exception to the Montana General Rule.

Concerns conduct that threatens or has some direct effect on the political integrity, the economic security, or the health or welfare of the tribe.

Narrowing the second exception [*see Strate v. A-1 Contractors, 520 U.S. 438 (1997)*]. The non-Indian conduct must have a direct nexus before the second exception in Montana will apply.

## WHAT CRIMINAL JX DO INDIAN TRIBES HAVE OVER NON-INDIANS, AND NON-MEMBER INDIANS IN INDIAN COUNTRY?

NON-INDIANS

**Before 1978:**

YES. Indian tribes had concurrent criminal JX with the federal government in non-PL-280 states or concurrent criminal JX with the states in a PL-280 state, over non-Indians who committed crimes in Indian country.

**After 1978, (*Oliphant*):**

NO. SCOTUS has imposed additional limitations on tribal authority by means of a judicially crafted theory that the Court has labeled the "Implicit Divestiture of [tribal] sovereignty." SCOTUS also decided that tribal courts do NOT have criminal JX over crimes in Indian country committed by non-Indian citizens of the U.S. Therefore, Indian tribes canNOT prosecute a non-Indian U.S. citizen, absent express Congressional authorization.

**After 2013, VAWA, a partial *Oliphant-fix*, up to March 6, 2015:**

YES. VAWA 2013 generally provided that Indian tribes can begin exercising special domestic violence criminal JX (SDVCJ) any time after March 7, 2015.

VAWA 2013 created a Pilot Project that authorized the U.S. Attorney

General to grant an Indian tribe's request to begin exercising SDVCJ earlier. Those three (3) tribes were: [1] Confederated Tribes of the Umatilla Indian Reservation; [2] Pascua Yaqui Tribe; and [3] Tulalip tribes.

VAWA amended the ICRA by expanding and partially overturning SCOTUS' decision in Oliphant. Oliphant held that tribal courts lacked criminal JX over non-Indian citizen defendants of the U.S.

However, in order to utilize this special domestic violence criminal JX, tribal courts shall have to provide certain enumerated due process protections. These include all of the TLOA 2010 due process protections, even if tribes do NOT impose the enhanced sentencing options, as well as several additional due process protections.

### After March 7, 2015, up to September 30, 2022:

YES. All Indian tribes may participate in implementing VAWA 2013. However, in order to utilize this special domestic violence criminal JX, tribal courts shall have to provide certain enumerated due process protections. These include all of the TLOA 2010 due process protections, even if tribes do NOT impose the enhanced sentencing options, as well as several additional due process protections.

### After October 1, 2022, up to the present:

YES. All Indian tribes have "special tribal criminal JX" over a broader range of "covered crimes," including assaulting tribal justice personnel, crimes of violence against children, stalking, protection order violations, sexual violence, sex trafficking, and obstruction of justice, among others. [See Pub. L. 117-103, Title VIII, §804. NOTE: With the passage of these amendments, tribes may now choose to exercise JX over additional crimes committed by non-Indians, provided they opt-in to the additional procedural protections. [See the ICRA of 1968 as amended].

## NON-MEMBER INDIANS

. . .

**Before 1885:**

YES. Concurrent JX with the federal government.

Federal pursuant to Title 28 of the revised statutes, §2145: all general laws of the U.S. apply to Indian country; exception §2146: [1] Indian against Indian, [2] Indian already punished by tribal law, or [3] Treaty provision of JX to the tribe.

**After 1885, up to through the stand-alone statutes, 1953, 1968, to the present in PL-280 States:**

YES. Concurrent JX with the states. Whereas, if the law was criminal and prohibitory in nature, then the state does have concurrent JX, pursuant to PL-280 to enforce their state criminal codes within Indian country.

**After 1885, up to 1990, in non-PL-280 States:**

YES. Concurrent JX with the federal government, but the tribes are limited to sentencing, pursuant to the ICRA of 1968, expanded sentencing, pursuant to the ICRA amended in 1986. NOTE: See the individual tribal constitution or statute for further limitations.

Federal JX over certain enumerated major crimes, the Indian Major Crimes Act, by all Indians in Indian country.

Tribes have exclusive JX over all other crimes NOT listed in the Indian Major Crimes Act.

**After 1990, *Duro v. Reina*, up to 1991:**

NO. An Indian tribe lacked inherent sovereign power to exercise criminal JX over non-member Indians is an "external power, inconsistent with the Indian tribe's dependent status, and thus capable of existing only by delegation from Congress, subject to the constraints of the Constitution."

SCOTUS limited the authority of tribal courts to punish non-member Indians. Therefore, Indian tribes have NO criminal JX over non-member Indians.

**After 1991, *Duro-fix*, up to 2004:**

YES. Congress overturned Duro by amending 25 USC §1301(2) and recognizing the inherent power of Indian tribes, "hereby recognized and affirmed," permitting tribal courts to exercise criminal JX over all Indians, NOT just member Indians.

**After 2004, *U.S. v. Lara*, up to 2010:**

YES. SCOTUS upheld Congress' reinstatement of inherent tribal criminal JX over non-member Indians, by way of the ICRA in 1991.

**After 2010, TLOA, up to 2013:**

YES. TLOA amended the ICRA by expanding the limitations on the term of imprisonment from one (1) year to three (3) years, and finds from five-thousand ($5,000) dollars to fifteen-thousand ($15,000) dollars, or both; or impose on a person in a criminal proceeding a total penalty or punishment greater than imprisonment for a term of nine (9) year; but only if certain additional requirements are met.

NOTE: TLOA did NOT amend or repeal the Indian Major Crimes Act.

————

## CRIMINAL JX AT A GLANCE – BACKGROUND CASES, AND STATUTES

1. *Worcester v. Georgia 31 U.S. (6 Pet.) 515 (1832)*

The supposedly "good Indian law" case. The most cited pre-civil war case. Indian tribes have traditionally had power "over both their members and their territory." Therefore, a tribe could exercise power over non-Indians and non-member Indians who entered reservation land. SCOTUS held that Georgia law had NO effect in Cherokee country even in the case of non-Indians. The history of tribal self-government forms the basis for the exercise of modern powers. Indian tribes consistently have been recognized first by the European nations. SCOTUS also held that the U.S. in Congress assembled, shall have the sole and exclusive right of regulating the trade with the Indian tribes and managing all their affairs [see the Indian Commerce Clause, Article 1, §8, Clause 3]. Congress is the appropriate body to deal with tribal nations. Plenary power doctrine: complete, total authority. Excludes state authority. Limited Judicial involvement. The Legislative power of the state is limited to citizens within the Legislative body's JX. NOTE: POTUS Jackson implemented the (voluntary) Indian Removal Act (1830) by forcing the five-civilized tribes to leave their ancestral homelands and march to present day Oklahoma.

SCOTUS limiting *Worcester*.

Non-Indian versus non-Indian, the now State has exclusive Jurisdiction [*see McBratney (1881)*]; and

Non-Indian versus Indian; the State now has concurrent Jurisdiction with the Federal Government [*see Oklahoma v. Castro-Huerta (2022)*].

NOTE: Is *Worcester* still good law?

## 2. *Ex-parte Crow Dog, 109 U.S. 556 (1883)*

The First Federal Indian Criminal Case. SCOTUS held that there is a strong affirmation of the principles of sovereignty and that Indian tribes possessed exclusive JX over crimes committed by one tribal member against another tribal member in Indian country and furthermore, that tribal members are therefore subject only to their tribal laws, unless the U.S. expressly states otherwise.

## 3. The Indian Major Crimes Act (1885)

Shortly, thereafter, and in response to the Crow Dog decision, Congress enacted 18 USCA §1153 – Indian Major Crimes Act; and §3242 – Indian committing certain offenses, acts on reservations. The FIRST STATUTE directly regulating internal tribal affairs by imposing criminal liability on Indians committing major crimes against other Indians within Indian country. Source of authority? Derived from the Indian Commerce Clause, Article 1, §8, Clause 3.

### 4. Lesser included offenses under 18 U.S.C. §1153

In *Keeble v. U.S., 412 U.S. 205 (1973)*, SCOTUS held that an Indian defendant charged with a major crime violation under 18 USCA §1153, was entitled to request and receive an instruction on a lesser included offense NOT enumerated in that section, even though the defendant could NOT have been charged with such an offense in the first instance.

### 5. *U.S. v. Kagama, 118 U.S. 375 (1886)*

SCOTUS has sustained the constitutionality of the Indian Major Crimes Act. SCOTUS canvassed the enumerated powers in the Constitution, finding each in turn insufficient. SCOTUS nevertheless upheld the MCA on two theories: [1] That only the U.S., as opposed to the states, is sovereign over the entire territory of the U.S.; and [2] That the U.S.'s role as the guardian of Indians, Indian tribes, and their property justifies any legislation enacted in this role of guardian. Therefore, according to SCOTUS, the Congress has absolute power over Indian tribes.

### 6. The Indian Civil Rights Act of 1968

The SECOND STATUTE directly regulating internal tribal affairs by imposing an Indian Bill of Rights. The ICRA contains several restrictions on Indian tribal governments. The Act extends many provisions in the Bill of Rights to individuals in their dealings with tribal governments. But judicial interpretation of the Act supports tribal autonomy, even in the face of claimed deprivations of important individual rights.

.   .   .

### 7. *Talton v. Mayes, 163 U.S. 376 (1896)*

There was only five people to the grand jury, grand jury are supposed to have at least six. This tribal grand jury was NOT up to U.S. Constitutional standards. Held that the 5TH Amendment does NOT apply because 1835 and 1868 Treaty; and tribes are pre-Constitutional.

NOTE: [See §1302(a)(D) 10. "deny to any person accused of an offense punishable by imprisonment the right, upon request, to a trial by jury of NOT less than six persons]."

The VAWA of 2013 amended the IRCA authorizing concurrent tribal JX over certain non-Indians for domestic, or dating violence crimes, or violation of proactive orders dealing with related conduct, in order to utilize this "special domestic violence criminal JX," tribal courts shall have to provide certain enumerated due process protections. These include all of the TLOA of 2010 due process protections, [even if tribes do NOT impose the enhanced sentencing options], as well as several additional due process protections including the right to an impartial jury.

### 8. *U.S. v. Wheeler, 435 U.S. 313 (1978)*

An Indian defendant can be prosecuted by two sovereigns, NO double jeopardy. As distinct, independent political communities, qualified to exercise powers of self-government, NOT by virtue of any delegation of powers, but rather by reason of their original tribal sovereignty.

### 9. Tribal, Federal, and State Jurisdiction

### Tribal jurisdiction

- If the perpetrator is a non-Indian, regardless of whether the victim is an Indian:
- *Oliphant v. Suquamish Indian Tribe, 435 U.S. 191 (1978).*

- SCOTUS has imposed additional limitations on tribal authority by means of a judicially crafted theory that the Court has labeled the "Implicit Divestiture of [tribal] sovereignty." SCOTUS also decided that tribal courts do NOT have criminal JX over crimes in Indian country committed by non-Indian citizens of the U.S. Therefore, Indian tribes canNOT prosecute a non-Indian citizen of the U.S., absent express Congressional authorization.
- If the perpetrator is Indian; and the victim is Indian:
- If the crime is NOT a major crime, hence, tribal criminal JX is exclusive.

## Federal jurisdiction

- If the perpetrator is a non-Indian; and the victim is Indian:
- If the crime violates either the federal criminal code or the criminal code of the states of occurrence, there is federal JX under the Indian Country Crimes Act.
- If the perpetrator is Indian; and the victim is Indian:
- If the crime is one of the enumerated major crimes, federal JX lies under the Major Crimes Act. If the crime is NOT a major crime, there is NO JX under either the Major Crimes Act or the Indian Country Crimes Act.

## State jurisdiction

- If the perpetrator is a non-Indian; and the victim is Indian:
- Prior to 2022, the state did NOT have criminal JX, unless PL-280.
- After July 2022, the state has concurrent JX with the Federal Government:
- Non-Indian versus Indian [see *Oklahoma v. Castro-Huerta*

(2022) *dramatically expanding the power of states to prosecute crimes in Indian country*]. SCOTUS upended two-hundred years of settled law regarding criminal jurisdiction in Indian country. The decision asserted that there is a presumption of state criminal jurisdiction that must be preempted in Indian country, undermining tribal sovereignty, and threatening safety and security for Indian people. Possible exceptions may include: [1] Treaty provisions; or [2] federal statutes.

- If the perpetrator is a non-Indian; and the victim is a non-Indian:
- There is exclusive state JX, [*see McBratney (1881) expanding the power of states to prosecute crimes in Indian country*].
- If there is NO victim?
- NOTE: Unclear, but both the state (pursuant to McBratney) and the federal government (pursuant to the ICCA) have exercised JX.
- If the perpetrator is Indian; and the victim is Indian:
- There is concurrent state JX with the tribes, pursuant to PL-280.

## 10. AMENDING THE ICRA of 1968 for the FIRST-TIME in 1986

The ICRA was amended for the first-time in 1986 in order to increase the sentencing limitations in section 1302(7). This provision originally limited tribes to imposing sentences for a single offense to NO greater than six (6) months imprisonment or a fine of five hundred ($500) dollars or both. In 1986, this provision was amended, as part of a federal drug and alcohol prevention Act, to read: "in no event impose for conviction of any one offense any penalty or punishment greater than imprisonment for a term of one (1) year or a fine of five thousand ($5,000) dollars or both."

## 11. Non-member Indian jurisdiction

*Duro v. Reina, 495 U.S. 676 (1990).*

SCOTUS extended the *Oliphant* holding in *Duro v. Reina*, and held that an Indian tribe also lacked inherent sovereign power to exercise criminal JX over non-member Indians, because it is an "external power inconsistent with the Indian tribe's dependent status" and thus capable of existing only "by delegation from Congress, subject to the constraints of the Constitution." SCOTUS limited the authority of tribal courts to punish non-member Indians. Therefore, Indian tribes have NO criminal JX over non-member Indians.

### 12. *Duro-Fix.* AMENDING THE ICRA of 1968 for the SECOND-TIME in 1991

The ICRA was amended for the second-time in 1991 in order to overturn the SCOTUS decision in *Duro v. Reina (1990)*. The Duro decision held that tribal courts lacked criminal JX over non-member Indians. The U.S. Congress overturned the Duro decision [the so-called Congressional Duro-fix] by adding language, "and means the inherent power of Indian tribes, hereby recognized and affirmed, to exercise criminal JX over all Indians," to the definition of "powers of self-government." This Congressional Duro-fix restored tribal court's inherent criminal JX over all Indians (members and non-members).

### 13. *U.S. v. Lara, 541 U.S. 193 (2004)*

SCOTUS ruled that double jeopardy did NOT apply to *LARA*, since the successive prosecutions were brought by separate and distinct sovereign bodies.

In 1990, SCOTUS ruled in *Duro v. Reina* that an Indian tribe did NOT have the authority to try an Indian criminally who was NOT a member of that tribe.

In 1991, Congress amended the ICRA to recognize that Indian tribes have the inherent sovereignty and authority to try non-member Indians for crimes committed within the tribe's territorial JX.

SCOTUS held that the Sovereign can do what he wants, and is NOT constrained by the Sovereign's Courts. We conclude that *DURO*, like several other cases, referred only to the need to obtain a Congressional statute that "delegate" power to the tribes. *See BOURLAND; and see also MONTANA.*

But in so stating, *DURO,* like the other cases, simply did NOT consider whether a statute, like the present one, could constitutionally achieve the same end by removing restrictions on the tribe's inherent authority. Consequently, we do NOT read any of these cases as holding that the Constitution forbids Congress to change "Judicially made" federal Indian law through this kind of Legislation. *See OLIPHANT.*

### 14. Tribal Law and Order Act of 2010. AMENDING THE ICRA of 1968 for the THIRD-TIME in 2010

The ICRA was amended for the third-time in 2010 by the passage of the Tribal Law and Order Act with the goal to improve public safety and justice systems in Indian country in response to significant rates of violent crime. Most notably, TLOA amends ICRA by expanding the limitations on the term of imprisonment from one (1) year to three (3) years, and fines from five-thousand ($5,000) dollars to fifteen-thousand ($15,000) dollars, that can be imposed on defendants convicted in tribal court. However, in order to impose these "enhanced sentencing" options of more than one (1) year on a defendant, tribal courts shall provide certain additional enumerated due process protections. These additional provisions include: "[1] provide to the defendant the right to effective assistance of counsel at least equal to that guaranteed by the U.S. Constitution; and [2] at the expense of the tribal government, provide an indigent defendant the assistance of a defense attorney licensed to practice law by any jurisdiction in the U.S. that applies appropriate professional licensing standards and effectively ensures the competence and professional responsibility of its licensed attorneys; [3] require that the judge presiding over the criminal proceeding (A) has sufficient legal training to preside over criminal proceedings; and (B) is licensed to practice law by any jurisdiction in the U.S.; [4] prior to charging the defendant, make publicly available the criminal laws (including regulations and interpretative documents), rules of evidence, and rules of criminal procedure (including rules governing the recusal of judges in appropriate circumstances) of the tribal government; and [5] maintain a record of the criminal proceeding, including an audio or other recording of the trial proceeding."

### 15. Violence Against Women Act of 2013. AMENDING THE ICRA of 1968 for the FOURTH-TIME in 2013

The ICRA was amended for the fourth-time in 2013 by the passage of the Violence Against Women Act in order to partially overturn the decision in Oliphant (tribal courts lacked criminal JX over non-Indian U.S. citizen defendants. Congress partially overturned the Oliphant decision in the re-authorization of VAWA 2013. Title IX of the VAWA Act, among other provisions, provided for "special domestic violence criminal JX" to tribal courts over non-Indian offenders who commit domestic violence, dating violence, or violate a protection order. Section 1304, added by the VAWA reauthorization, recognizes tribal criminal JX over non-Indians committing various covered crimes against Indians in Indian country. These crimes include domestic and sexual violence as well as violent crimes against children and sex trafficking, among others. Tribes may also exercise criminal JX over certain other covered crimes, such as assault of tribal justice personnel or obstruction of tribal justice even where neither the defendant nor the victim are Indian. [See §1304(b)(4). Defendants must be granted all of the protections of §1302(b) the extended sentences.

However, in order for Congress to recognize and affirm the inherent power of the participating tribe to exercise special domestic violence criminal JX over the non-Indian defendant, tribal courts shall have to provide all other rights whose protection is necessary under the Constitution of the U.S.

These include all of the TLOA of 2010 due process protections, even if the participating tribe does NOT impose the enhanced sentencing options, as well as several additional due process protections, including: "[3] the right to a jury by an impartial jury that is drawn from sources that [A] reflect a fair cross section of the community; and [B] do NOT systematically exclude any distinctive group in the community, including non-Indians."

NOTE: *Oklahoma v. McGirt (2020)*, McGirt a non-member Indian affirmed the inherent right of tribal nations to exercise criminal JX to protect native victims against native perpetrators across all tribal lands.

NOTE: *Oklahoma v. Castro-Huerta (2022)*, a non-Indian had been charged with criminal neglect with regards to his stepdaughter, a citizen of the Eastern Band of Cherokee Indians. Castro-Huerta committed his crime against a Cherokee child, within the borders of the Cherokee Nation. However, instead of discussing the sovereign interest a tribal nation maintains to protect a child citizen, Justice Kavanaugh wrote the 5-4 majority opinion, and justified his decision to grant the state criminal JX over the crime based on the premise that the only parties to the criminal case are the state, and the non-Indian defendant. NOTE: Nowhere in the Court's majority opinion was consideration for the rights of a native child to be protected by her own tribal nation; a right that Congress recently restored in the 2022 reauthorization of VAWA. NOTE: There is NO law here, just pure political preference. NO lower federal court issued a ruling. The case was moot. There was NO split decisions in the circuits. SCOTUS plucked it, with an express purpose to change the law in Indian country in a way that SCOTUS preferred.

## THE CLEAR AS MUD, ANALYTICAL APPROACH TO FEDERAL CRIMINAL JURISDICTION IN INDIAN COUNTRY

Insert a Hypothetical Fact Pattern here.

Indian Perpetrator

- Who was the victim? (PERSON)
- Member Indian
- Non-member Indian
- Non-Indian
- What was the Crime? (CRIME)
- Jurisdiction. Where did the crime occur? (PLACE)

- Federal
- State
- Tribal

Non-Indian Perpetrator

- Who was the victim? (PERSON)
- Member Indian
- Non-member Indian
- Non-Indian
- What was the Crime? (CRIME)
- Jurisdiction. Where did the crime occur? (PLACE)
- Federal
- State
- Tribal

––––––

1. Was the Locus (location) of the crime in Indian country?
2. Does Public Law 280, or a specific jurisdictional statute apply?
3. Was the crime committed by, or against an Indian?
4. Which defendant – victim category applies?
5. Crimes by an Indian against an Indian.
6. Crimes by and Indian against a non-Indian.
7. Crimes by a non-Indian against an Indian.
8. Crimes by a non-Indian against a non-Indian.
9. Victimless, and consensual crimes by an Indian. NOTE: In theory, the tribal court should only have jurisdiction, but in practice, the federal court applies the assimilated crimes act.
10. Victimless, and consensual crimes by a non-Indian. NOTE: In theory, the federal court should only have jurisdiction, but because of the ruling in U.S. v. McBratney, the state court assumes jurisdiction, even though they do NOT have it.

FINAL TAKE-AWAYS

**Federal Indian law (the make no sense law)**

Look to the 400 + Treaties between the United States and the various Tribes. Also, look to the federal statutes, aka Acts (that have been passed by both houses of Congress, the Senate (100 Senators), and the House of Representatives (435 Reps); Executive Orders (POTUS); Rules and Regulations established by the various Departments such as the Bureau of Indian Affairs (BIA) under the Department of the Interior; the Indian Health Services (IHS) under the Department of Health and Human Services; and the common law Doctrines created by SCOTUS.

NOTE: If POTUS started a treaty process, and negotiated a deal with an Indian tribe, and the SENATE ratified it, then it would be a valid a treaty, in spite of the 1871 Act. As a practical matter, the treaty era never ended. [For example see since the 1970s, every Indian tribe negotiates an annual funding agreement with the U.S. federal government (as a matter of law), and are renegotiated every-year, in light of the Indian self-determination era, effectively are treaties].

## THE TWO-SIDES OF THE TRIBAL SOVEREIGNTY COIN:

**On the one side of the coin, it reads:**

"Whatever has NOT been taken away, remains." Felix Cohen.

NOTE: This is the Retained Tribal Sovereignty.

NOTE: In 1790, the U.S. Congress preempted the field of Indian law by passing the Trade and Intercourse Act. Nobody can go into Indian country, without the permission of Congress. NOTE: The general rule: States have NO power in Indian country, unless Congress gives it to them.

**On the flip side of the coin, it reads:**

"Whatever has NOT been delegated, by the United States to the tribes has been taken away." SCOTUS after *OLIPHANT*.

NOTE: This is the Retained, Dependent, Implicit Divestiture, of Tribal Sovereignty.

NOTE: The NEW general rule (2022): States have NO power in Indian country, unless Congress gives it to them; or SCOTUS decides, if they have that power.

## NATIVE AMERICAN INDIAN TRIBES HAVE JURISDICTION OVER:

(MEMBER INDIANS): Retained diminished inherent tribal sovereignty over its own members. [*See Worcester v. Georgia (1832); Indian Major Crimes Act (1885); and ICRA (1968)*].

(NON-MEMBER INDIAN): Retained diminished, re-recognized inherent tribal sovereignty over non-member Indians. [*See Indian Major Crimes Act (1885); Duro v. Reina (1990); and ICRA (1991)*].

(NON-INDIAN): Implicit Divestiture with delegation from the U.S. Congress, retained but dependent delegation of tribal sovereignty over non-Indians when regulating its internal affairs stripped away over time by the U.S. federal government by Treaties, POTUS Executive Orders, regulations, Congressional Statutes, and SCOTUS common law decisions. [*See Suquamish Tribe v. Oliphant (1978); U.S. v. Montana (1981); Doctrine of Discovery inside Johnson v. McIntosh (1823); TLOA (2010); and VAWA (2013), and (2022)*].

**KEY TERMS:**

- Indian law
- Federal Indian law
- Indian
- Non-member Indian

- Non-Indian
- Indian country
- Treaties
- Congressional Statutes
- Executive Orders/Rules and Regulations
- Supreme Court Opinions and Doctrines
- The Indian Commerce Clause
- The Doctrine of Discovery
- Indian Title
- Domestic Dependent Nation
- Diminished Sovereignty
- The Plenary Powers Doctrine
- The Trust Doctrine
- The Canons of Construction Doctrine
- The Department of War/Department of Interior/Bureau of Indian Affairs
- The Code of Federal Regulations/Courts/Police
- The Indian Major Crimes Act
- The General Allotment Act
- The Doctrine of Indian Water Rights
- The Indian Reorganization Act
- The Indian Relocation Act
- The Public Law 280 Act
- Civil/adjudicatory/regulatory/Jurisdiction
- The Infringement Test
- The Indian Civil Rights Act
- The Indian Self-Determination and Assistance Act
- Criminal Jurisdiction
- Delegation
- Inherent Sovereignty
- Double Jeopardy
- The Dual Sovereignty
- Forum Shopping
- The Indian Child Welfare Act
- Fee land/trust land/restricted trust land/unrestricted trust land

- The Indian Gaming Regulatory Act
- The Doctrine of Sovereign Immunity
- Tribal Law and Order Act
- Violence Against Women Act
- Personal Jurisdiction
- Territorial Jurisdiction
- Subject Matter Jurisdiction
- Nation Building
- The Retained Tribal Sovereignty
- The Retained Dependent Implicit Divestiture Tribal Sovereignty

## A CALL-TO-ACTION GUIDE WITH THE BOOK:

**The Quick-Action Steps:**

[momentum builder]; [confidence builder]; [progression]; [personal development]; [a push for action]; and [just do it right now].

- 1. Write a "why" statement clearly explaining the reason you desire to be a leader, and how you are going to apply it to your life?
- 2. What is something that you wish somebody would have told you that could have launched you closer and/-or sooner towards your goals?
- 3. What is your old surviving belief; and what is your new thriving belief you have about yourself?

**Create Your Vision:**

[clarify is specific] [imagine the first-step]; and [remain focused].

1. What are three goals that you want to achieve today?
2. What are three goals that you want to achieve in three months?
3. What are three goals that you want to achieve in six months?

4. What are three goals that you want to achieve in one year?
5. What are three goals that you want to achieve in three years?
6. What are three goals that you want to achieve in five years?
7. What are three goals that you want to achieve in ten years?
8. Why are (1-7) a must?
9. What has kept you from changing (1-7) in the past?
10. What needs to change (1-7) now?
11. What are the 1-2 actionable steps that will immediately move your goals (1-7) forward?

**General Questions Posed from reading this chapter:**

1. Give four-ways in which you can relate to this chapter?
2. Research and write a reflection paper on four-different topics found in this chapter.

**Specific Questions Posed from reading this chapter:**

1. Analyze the federal jurisdiction prosecutorial criminal authority for crimes committed by an Indian against an Indian in Indian country. Explain.
2. Analyze the federal jurisdiction prosecutorial criminal authority for crimes committed by an Indian against a non-Indian in Indian country. Explain.
3. Analyze the federal jurisdiction prosecutorial criminal authority for crimes committed by a non-Indian against an Indian in Indian country. Explain.
4. Analyze the federal jurisdiction prosecutorial criminal authority for crimes committed by a non-Indian against a non-Indian in Indian country. Explain.

# THE AUTHOR'S RECOMMENDED READINGS

BOOKS

*Introduction to Tribal Legal Studies*, 3$^{rd}$ edition, by Justin B. Richland and Sarah Deer, Lanham, MD: Rowman & Littlefield, (2016); ISBN No. 978-1-4422-3224-2.

*The nations within: The past and future of American Indian sovereignty*, by Deloria V. Jr., and Lytle, CM, (1998); ISBN No. 0394725662.

*The death and rebirth of the Seneca*, by Wallace AFC, Random House (1970); ISBN No. 039471699X.

*Federal Indian Law and Policy an Introduction*, by Keith Richotte, Jr., West Academic Publishing (2020); ISBN No. 978-1-64242-605-2.

*Like a Loaded Weapon, the Rehnquist Court, Indian Rights, and the Legal History of Racism in America*, by Robert A. Williams, Jr., University of Minnesota Press (2005); ISBN No. 0-8166-4709-7.

*Concise Hornbooks, Principles of Federal Indian Law*, by Matthew L.M. Fletcher, West Academic Publishing (2017); ISBN No. 978-1-63460-623-3.

*Federal Indian Law*, by Matthew L.M. Fletcher, Hornbook Series, West Academic Publishing (2016); ISBN No. 978-0-314-29071-7.

*Discovering Indigenous Lands, The Doctrine of Discovery in the English Colonies*, by Robert J. Mill, Jacinta Ruru, Larissa Behrendt, and Tracey Lindberg, Oxford University Press (2010); ISBN No. 978-0-19-965185-6.

*The Indian Civil Rights Act at Forty*, edited by Kristen A. Carpenter, Matthew L.M. Fletcher, and Angela R. Riley, The Regents of the University of California (2012); ISBN No. 0-935626-67-0.

*The Rights of Indians and Tribes, Fourth Edition*, by Stephen L. Pevar, Oxford University Press (2012) ISBN No. 978-0-19-979535-2.

*Reading American Indian Law, Foundational Principles*, edited by Grant Christensen and Melissa L. Tatum, Cambridge University Press, University Printing House (2020); ISBN No. 9781108488532.

*Indian Law Stories*, edited by Carole Goldberg, Kevin K. Washburn, and Philip P. Frickey, Foundation Press (2011); ISBN No. 978-1-59941-729-5.

*The Indian Child Welfare Act Handbook, A Legal Guide to the Custody and Adoption of Native American Children, Second Edition*, by BJ Jones,

Mark Tilden, and Kelly Gaines-Stoner, American Bar Association; ISBN No. 978-1-59031-858-7.

*Indian Gaming Law & Policy, Second Edition,* by Kathryn R.L. Rand, and Steven Andrew Light, Carolina Academic Press (2014); ISBN No. 978-1-59460-956-5.

*Labor and Employment Law in Indian Country, 2011 Edition,* by Kaighn Smith, Jr., Native American Rights Fund, (2011); ISBN No. 978-0-9794099-9-8.

Cases and Materials on Federal Indian Law, Seventh Edition, by David H. Getches, Charles F. Wilkinson, Robert A. Williams, Jr., Matthew L.M. Fletcher, and Kristen A. Carpenter, West Academic Publishing, (2017); ISBN No. 978-1-63459-906-1.

*American Indian Law in a nutshell, Sixth Edition,* by William C. Canby, Jr., West Nutshell Series, West Academic Publishing, (2015); ISBN No. 978-1-62810-008-2.


ARTICLES

*There and Back Again—An Indian Hobbit's Holiday: Indians Teaching Indian Law,* by G. William "Bill" Rice, University of Tulsa College of Law, TU Law Digital Commons, (1996).

*The Indian Law Bombshell: McGirt v. Oklahoma,* by Robert J. Miller, and Torey Dolan, Boston University Law Review (2021).

*Tribal Law and Order Act: Enhanced Sentencing Authority, Tribal Code Development Considerations Quick-Reference Overview and Checklist,* authored by Michelle Rivard Parks, contributions by Deborah Flute, Tribal Judicial Institute, University of North Dakota School of Law (2015).

*Taking Stock: Open Questions and Unfinished Business Under the VAWA Amendments to the Indian Civil Rights Act,* by Jordan Gross, Faculty Law Review Article (2022).

*Santa Clara Pueblo v. Martinez in the Evolution of Federal Law,* by Richard B. Collins, Tribal Law Journal, Vol. 20, Article 1 (2021).

*Incorporation by any other name? Comparing Congress' Federalization of Tribal Court Criminal Procedure with the Supreme Court's Regulation of*

*State Courts*, by Jordan Gross, Kentucky Law Journal, Vol. 109, No. 299 (2020).

*The Rise of Tribes and the Fall of Federal Indian Law*, by Lance Morgan, Arizona State Law Journal (2017).

*"Whatever Tribal Precedent There May Be": The (Un)availability of Tribal Law*, by Bonnie Shucha, Law Library Journal, Vol. 106:2 (2014).

*The Sky Will Not Fall in Oklahoma*, by Clint Summers, Tulsa Law Review, Vol. 56, Issue 3 (2021).

*The Other American Law*, by Elizabeth A. Reese, Stanford Law Review, Vol. 73, (2021).

*The Bureau of Indian Affairs and the Federal Trust Obligation to American Indians*, by Robert McCarthy, Brigham Young University Journal of Public Law, Volume 19, No. 1 (2004).

*Federal Criminal Law and Tribal Self-Determination*, by Kevin K. Washburn, North Carolina Law Review, Vol. 84, No. 3 (2006).

*Implicit Divestiture Reconsidered: Outtakes from the Cohen's Handbook Cutting-Room Floor*, by John P. LaVelle, Connecticut Law Review, Vol. 38, No. 4 (2006).

*The Supreme Court and Federal Indian Policy*, by Matthew L.M. Fletcher, Nebraska Law Review, Vol. 85, No. 1 (2006).

*Politics, History, and Semantics: The Federal Recognition of Indian Tribes*, by Matthew L.M. Fletcher, North Dakota Law Review, Vol. 82, No. 2 (2006).

*The Pedagogy of American Indian Law*, North Dakota Law Review, Vol. 82., No. 3 (2006).

*Water Rights, Water Quality, and Regulatory Jurisdiction in Indian country*, by Robert T. Anderson, 34 Stan. Envtl. L.J. 195, 204 (2015).

*Case Law on American Indians*, by Thomas P. Schlosser, American Indian Law Journal, Vol. 10, Iss. 2, Art 1 (2022).

# CHAPTER 2
# HOW TO BECOME LEARNED IN TRIBAL GOVERNMENT AND LAW

## [A] WHAT IS TRIBAL LAW?

To date, there are 574 federally recognized American Indian and Alaska Native Nations in the United States. Although there are a lot of similarities between each tribal nation, each tribal nation is unique in their own ways. Each tribal nation has their own unique oral, and written history, ceremony, language, customs, traditions, values, beliefs, norms, structures, practices and laws.

## [B] WHO IS AN INDIGENOUS PERSON?

Legally and politically, an American Indian is an enrolled member of a federally recognized tribe by the United States Government.

When referring to an individual Indigenous person, rather than as "American Indian or Native American," tribes refer to themselves in their own names, such as Anishanaabe, Nehiyahw, or Dine.

## [C] WHAT ARE INDIAN RESERVATIONS, AND HOW ARE THEY ESTABLISHED/CREATED?

Answer: A reservation is a territory reserved by tribes as a permanent tribal homeland. Reservations were created through Treaties with the U.S.; Statutes; or Executive Orders

The definition of an Indian reservation, like the definition of an Indian, is complicated by social, historical, political, and legal factors. There are federally and state recognized reservations. A reservation is land that is set aside for the use by Indians. Also see the historical/legal origins, federal attacks on the land base, white residence fee lands within the exterior boundaries of the reservation, and the jurisdictional issues over reservation residents and their property.

## [D] HOW ARE INDIAN RESERVATIONS DISESTABLISHED, AND BY WHAT BRANCH OF U.S. THE FEDERAL GOVERNMENT?

Answer: Even though some reservations were established through a statute, executive order, or treaty (and with Treaties there is no mechanism in the Constitution to abrogate treaties and Treaties are named in the U.S. Constitution as the supreme law of the land, SCOTUS has repeatedly stated that Congress has the sole plenary power regulating Indian affairs. Therefore, only Congress may diminish and/-or disestablish the exterior boundaries of any Indian reservation, and its intent to do so must be clear. *(See Nebraska v. Parker (2016) citing Solem v. Bartlett (1984).* You look at the actual language of the statute. NOTE Step 1 of 3 in the *Solem v. Bartlett* case solves the issue in the *McGirt v. Oklahoma* case. *[See McGirt v. Oklahoma (2020)].*

## [E] WHAT IS THE SOURCE OF TRIBAL LAW?

The source of an Indian tribe's power is its people. Indian tribes and their members have the inherent right to govern themselves, a right they have possessed from time immemorial.

In a legal and governmental context sovereignty can be defined as the absolute and independent right to make one's own laws, rules, or regulations and to be governed by the same. To this end tribal governments retain this same absolute right to make laws and to be governed by them, subject only to the plenary power of the federal government. Tribes are thus trying to delicately balance the management of their own affairs with the scrutiny of outside jurisdiction, a difficult balance knowing that federal assertion of plenary power could, at any time, interfere with that exercise.

As the federal appellate court stated, Indian tribes are neither states, nor part of the federal government, nor subdivisions of either. Rather they are sovereign political entities possessed of sovereign authority not derived from the United States, which they predate. [Indian tribes are] qualified to exercise powers of self-government...by reason of their original tribal sovereignty, *National Labor Relations Board v. Pueblo of San Juan, (10th Cir. 2002) citing Worcester v. Georgia (1832).*

In its simplest form, tribal sovereignty is the ability of a people to make their own local laws and be ruled only by those local laws. NOTE: Post-Castro-Huerta (2022), seems as if SCOTUS would support states' rights to pass laws that tribes oppose; and the barrier to state power would not be tribal sovereignty, and express treaty rights; but instead, whether a case-by-case federal preemption analysis would keep the state at bay.

## [F] WHAT ARE THE LIMITS OF TRIBAL POWER?

SCOTUS has consistently held that although Indian tribes have inherent sovereign powers, Congress has plenary authority to limit, modify, or eliminate the powers of local self-government which the tribes otherwise possess. *U.S. v. Lara (2004).*

This is a principle of law that is ultimately based on military power. Indian tribes have two-types of limitations on their governmental powers:

## 1. EXPRESS

The U.S. Congress has expressly prohibited Indian tribes from exercising certain powers, such as selling tribal lands without the federal government's permission, and limiting incarcerating someone in tribal jail for more than six months for any one offense, and/-or fine up to $500 (ICRA of 1968).

See the Indian Major Crimes Act (1885); the Indian Reorganization Act (1934); and the Termination era.

Many educational programs and services were transferred from the Department of Interior, Bureau of Indian Affairs to the Departments of Health, Education, and Welfare. See the Indian Civil Rights Act (1968); and its four amendments Anti-Drug Abuse Act (1986); *Duro-fix* (1991); TOLA (2010); and VAWA (2013).

## 2. IMPLIED

Indian tribes have lost many of the attributes of sovereignty by implication. SCOTUS held due to their dependent status that is, by virtue of their incorporation. *See Oliphant v. Suquamish Tribe (1978).*

Indian tribes may no longer declare war on a foreign government or exercise certain powers over non-Indians.

Indian tribes have impliedly lost those powers due to their subordinate position as conquered or purchased nations under the control of the federal government.

NOTE: However, those powers not expressly removed by Congress or lost by implication are retained (reserved) by the Indian tribe. (EX) The Reserved Rights Doctrine.

## [G] WHAT ARE THE CHARACTERISTICS AND LEGAL DOCUMENTS OF TRIBAL GOVERNMENT?

### TIME IMMEMORIAL

Tribal nations have oral and traditional customs, spiritual, and written laws to govern internal tribal relations, external relations, commercial relations, and all interaction between tribal members and the rest of the world.

### CONTEMPORARY

Tribal nations have written laws, codified some customs and traditions, or parts of state laws.

See Tribal Constitution or Statute establishing the government and the governing body, power to adopt statutes, ordinances, resolutions, subject to the approval of the United States Secretary of Interior or as delegated, or removed (see specific tribal document).

1. Tribal Constitution or Statute.
2. Statutes/Acts/Ordinances/Resolutions.
3. Policies and Procedures/Promulgated Rules.
4. Judicial Appellate decisions, caselaw interpreting the tribal constitution, statutes, ordinances, and/-or resolutions.

TEMPLATE CONSTITUTION (Sovereign tribes engaging settler governments).

Typically a tribal government in developing its government by either constitution or statute will provide for [1] a preamble; [2] a definition of its territory and jurisdiction; [3] membership; [4] organization of the government: tribal council aka business committee; or powers of the tribal council made up of the membership over eighteen years of age; powers of the legislative branch; powers of the executive branch; and powers of the judicial branch; [5] tribal administration; [6] elections; [7] removal, recall, and vacancy of tribal officials; [8] administration of land provisions; [9] initiative and referendums; [10] adoption of ordinances and resolutions; [11] sovereign immunity; [12] bill of rights; [13] general meetings; [14] amendments; [15] savings clause; [16] certification of results of election; and [17] adoption of constitution or statute.

NOTE: These are generally the more important constitutional or statutory provisions. There are others which are contained in various sample constitutions or statutes that can easily be researched and written for a specific tribe to adopt or amend. Keep in mind, these provisions are intended to be samples, and are NOT provisions required by the U.S. Secretary of Interior. In the development of a tribal constitution or statute, a tribe may promulgate provisions that are tailored to meet their specific needs and/-or requirements, so long as they are NOT in violation of federal law. Please contact the author of this book if you are seeking technical assistance to develop new constitutional or statutory provisions, or revise an existing constitution or statute.

## TRIBAL SOVEREIGNTY

To fully understand JX within Indian country, you need to understand the legal theory of sovereignty in federal Indian law. Perhaps the most fundamental concept within Indian law is that tribes are sovereign governments. That is, tribes possess powers of self-government that pre-exist the formation of the U.S. Here are the main attributes of tribal sovereignty:

[1] Tribal sovereignty is inherent, meaning that it exists separately from any delegation by the federal government. Tribes are therefore separate sovereigns from the U.S. or the states;

[2] As a separate sovereign, a tribe is NOT subject to the restrictions of the Bill of Rights in the U.S. Constitution. They are however, subject to similar restrictions under the ICRA of 1968 and its amendments; and tribal statutes; or constitutions creating a bill of rights for those subject to their governmental authority; and

[3] While tribes have inherent sovereignty, such sovereignty is limited within the federal system. SCOTUS coined the term Domestic Dependent Nations to describe the status of tribes within the U.S. The theory is that tribes sought the protection of the U.S. by entering into treaties with it and by doing so implicitly surrendered the full sovereignty they previously possessed.

·  ·  ·

[H] INTRODUCTION TO THE LEGAL HISTORY OF TRIBAL POLICE, AND THE COURTS

During the allotment era, the federal government established Indian police forces and Indian courts on several reservations. Staffed by tribal members themselves, both the police and the courts were extensions of the efforts to civilize Native peoples.

THE INDIAN POLICE (INSTRUMENTS OF CULTURAL OPPRESSION)
   The Indian police were created to enforce American law and the rules and regulations established by the Indian agent, who would later become the superintendent, or field agent.

1824. The Bureau of Indian Affairs (previously the office of Indian Affairs, originated in the Department of War, then the Department of Defense, then moved into the Department of Interior) has changed dramatically over the past 185 years, evolving as Federal policies designed to subjugate, and assimilate American Indians and Alaska Natives, to policies that promote Indian self-determination.

## THE COURTS OF INDIAN OFFENSES (INSTRUMENTS OF CULTURAL OPPRESSION)

1878. Congress approved the establishment of the federal Indian police and by 1890 nearly all reservations had them.

1883. Department of Interior established the rules of Indian courts. Code of Federal Regulations [Title 25, Chapter 1, Subchapter B, Part 11, Courts of Indian Offenses and Law and Order Code].

. . .

Indian courts were created to punish those who ran afoul of American law, and/-or the Indian agent's rules, who would later become the superintendent, or field agent. The Indian courts established in this era are sometimes referred to as CFR courts, because their guidelines were codified in Title 25, of the 51 Titles that are found in the Code of Federal Regulations. Some tribal nations continue to operate CFR courts today, although they have much greater control over them now than they did during the allotment era.

Courts of Indian offenses to prosecute tribal members had more to do with suppressing religious dances and certain kinds of ceremonies than with keeping law and order; and prosecuted for practicing his or her traditional religion such as the Sun Dance, aka the Thirst Dance, sweatlodge, engaging in traditional dancing, NOT dipping your sheep in oil, or cohabitating without being married under Western law. The U.S. sought to replace these ancient spiritual practices with Christianity. The court is one of various methods that the U.S. employs to try to restrict the cultural identity of American Indian tribes. Many, political, cultural, and spiritual leaders were imprisoned.

Many of the offenses handled by the police and the courts in the allotment era were common crimes, such as theft. However, as they were tools of oppression, acculturation, and assimilation of the push toward civilization, both the BIA police, and the CFR courts often punished those who violated the ethos of the progress, the federal government sought to instill within reservations.

The Indian agent, superintendent, or field agent held great sway over the police and the courts, sometimes accompanying police during arrests, appointing judges, or even acting as the chief of police, and the chief judge themselves.

## 1888. SEE UNITED STATES V. CLAPOX, 35 F. 575, 577 (D.OR. 1888)

- Federal Policing authorized by federal statutes
- State Policing authorized by PL-280
- Tribal Policing authorized by PL-638; Self-Compact; and Inherent tribal sovereignty

----

**Administered by**

- Federal government. DOI/BIA/LES
- State government
- Tribal government

**Officers employed by**

- BIA police are employees of the federal government with union protections.
- State police are employees of the State with union protections.
- Tribal police are employees of the tribal government.

**Primary source of funding**

- Congressional authorizations, with line-item direct services.
- State governments, with some federal support through federal grants to states and municipalities.
- Federal funding from the Department of Interior; Department of Justice; block grants to the tribes; or full funding by the tribes.

In the pre-reservation days, the failure of a tribal police society to carry out its duty would have meant the failure of the hunt for the whole tribe and raise the prospect of starvation. Today, the strength and health of Indian communities is NO less dependent on the maintenance of safety and justice by Indian judges and law enforcement personnel.

The men and women who hold the gavel, or wear the badge in the

Indian criminal justice system today are charged with an awesome responsibility to carry on the work of those who came before. From Chief Spotted Tail of the Dakota's tribal and BIA police and corrections, tribal trial court judges, tribal appellate court justices, state court judges and justices, federal district court judges, appellate court justices, to SCOTUS, the importance of the Indian criminal justice system has long been recognized. We must continue to improve the quality and efficiency of our work to better safeguard our Native communities and maintain the honor of our heritage.

## FINAL TAKE-AWAYS

### Tribal Government and law

Traditional clan and kinship system, shifted to constitutional or statute modern governments.

Look to Constitutions or Statutes establishing the Tribal Government; acts/ordinances (making laws consistent with the Constitution or Statute); highest appellate case law (determining whether or not the act/ordinance/code/policy is constitutional or statutory or not); policies and procedures for each branch of government; promulgated rules written by commissions and/-or boards subject to a higher authority [(ex) Legislature, Governor/President/Chairperson, business committee/also called the tribal council, executive directors, directors].

1491. Inherent Tribal Sovereignty. In its simple form, sovereignty is the ability of a people to make their own laws and live by them. The source of an Indian tribe's power is its people. Indian tribes and their members have the inherent right to govern themselves, a right they have possessed "from time immemorial."

1832. Inherent Diminished Dependent Sovereignty.

. . .

1978. Implicit Divestiture Retained Dependent Sovereignty.

Treaty provisions and statutory Acts are administered directly by the federal agencies, or contracted through self-compact or 638 contracts that are operated by the specific tribe's governing body.

## THE TWO-SIDES OF THE TRIBAL SOVEREIGNTY COIN:

**On the one side of the coin, it reads:**
   "Whatever has NOT been taken away, remains." Felix Cohen.
   NOTE: This is the Retained Tribal Sovereignty.

**On the flip side of the coin, it reads:**
   "Whatever has NOT been delegated, by the United States to the tribes has been taken away." SCOTUS after *OLIPHANT*.
   NOTE: This is the Retained, Dependent, Implicit Divestiture, of Tribal Sovereignty.

**KEY TERMS:**

   - Tribal law
   - Indian
   - Reservations
   - Tribal government
   - Contemporary tribal government documents
   - Tribal Constitution
   - Tribal sovereignty
   - Tribal police
   - Tribal courts
   - Inherent Tribal Sovereignty
   - Inherent Diminished Dependent Sovereignty

- Implicit Divestiture Retained Dependent Sovereignty

## A CALL-TO-ACTION GUIDE WITH THE BOOK

### The Quick-Action Steps:
[momentum builder]; [confidence builder]; [progression]; [personal development]; [a push for action]; and [just do it right now].

1. Write a "why" statement clearly explaining the reason you desire to be a leader, and how you are going to apply it to your life?
2. What is something that you wish somebody would have told you that could have launched you closer and /-or sooner towards your goals?
3. What is your old surviving belief; and what is your new thriving belief you have about yourself?

### Create Your Vision:
[clarify is specific] [imagine the first-step]; and [remain focused].

1. What are three goals that you want to achieve today?
2. What are three goals that you want to achieve in three months?
3. What are three goals that you want to achieve in six months?
4. What are three goals that you want to achieve in one year?
5. What are three goals that you want to achieve in three years?
6. What are three goals that you want to achieve in five years?
7. What are three goals that you want to achieve in ten years?
8. Why are (1-7) a must?
9. What has kept you from changing (1-7) in the past?
10. What needs to change (1-7) now?
11. What are the 1-2 actionable steps that will immediately move your goals (1-7) forward?

**General Questions Posed from reading this chapter:**

1. Give four-ways in which you can relate to this chapter?
2. Research and write a reflection paper on four-different topics found in this chapter.

**Specific Questions Posed from reading this chapter:**

1. In your community, what year was your reservation created and how (by Treaty, by Act, by Executive Order)? Explain.
2. In your community, what legal documents can be available, where and how for review, and/-or copy? Explain.
3. In your community, how many branches of government are there by constitution, by statute (1, 2, 3, or 4)? Explain.
4. Should each branch of the tribal government be bound by a code of ethics? Explain.
5. In your community what is the structure of the police (BIA, tribal police, state police, or combination)? Explain.
6. In your community what is the structure of the courts (CFR, tribal courts, state courts)? Explain.
7. How should a tribal court apply the concept of "due process," implicitly or explicitly? Explain.
8. How should tribal courts determine what interests require due process and, once identified, decide what process is appropriate? Explain.
9. How should a tribal court adopt federal interpretations of due process, applying United States Supreme Court precedent and tests, and merely predict what the outcome would be were a federal court to rule on the issue? Explain.
10. How should a tribal court attempt to find unique tribal ways of thinking about due process, developing its own

jurisprudence based on the customs, traditions, and public policy of the tribe regardless of federal rulings? Explain.

11. Analyze the tribal jurisdiction prosecutorial criminal authority for crimes committed by an Indian against an Indian in Indian country. Explain.

12. Analyze the tribal jurisdiction prosecutorial criminal authority for crimes committed by an Indian against a non-Indian in Indian country. Explain.

13. Analyze the tribal jurisdiction prosecutorial criminal authority for crimes committed by a non-Indian against an Indian in Indian country. Explain.

14. Analyze the tribal jurisdiction prosecutorial criminal authority for crimes committed by a non-Indian against a non-Indian in Indian country. Explain.

## THE AUTHOR'S RECOMMENDED READINGS

BOOKS

*Introduction to Tribal Legal Studies, 3rd edition*, by Justin B. Richland and Sarah Deer, Lanham, MD: Rowman & Littlefield (2016); ISBN No. 978-1-4422-3224-2.

*Rebuilding Native Nations: Strategies for Governance and Development*, edited by Miriam Jorgensen, The University of Arizona Press (2007); ISBN No. 978-0-8165-2421-1.

*Tribal Government Today, Politics on Montana Indian Reservations, Revised Edition*, by James J. Lopach, Margery Hunter Brown, and Richmond L. Clow; University Press of Colorado (1998); ISBN No. 0-87081-477-X.

*North Dakota Indians, an Introduction, Second Edition*, by Mary Jane Schneider, Kendall/Hunt Publishing Company, (1994); ISBN No. 0-8403-9615-5.

*American Indian Tribal Governments*, by Sharon O'Brien, University of Oklahoma Press (1989); ISBN No. 0-8061-2199-8.

*American Indians, American Justice*, by Vine Deloria, Jr., and Clifford M. Lytle, University of Texas Press, (1983); ISBN No. 978-0-292-73834-8.

*A Sovereign People*, by Leo K. Killsback, Texas Tech University Press (2020); ISBN No. 978-1-68283-037-6.

*A Sacred People*, by Leo K. Killsback, Texas Tech University Press (2020); ISBN No. 978-1-68283-035-2.

*The Cherokee Supreme Court: 1823-1835*, by J. Matthew Martin, Carolina Academic Press (2021); ISBN No. 978-1-5310-1841-2.

*American Indian Tribal Law, Second Edition*, by Matthew L.M. Fletcher, Wolters Kluwer, Aspen Coursebook Series (2020); ISBN No. 978-1-5438-1364-7.

*Mastering American Indian Law, Second Edition*, by Angelique Wambdi Eaglewoman, and Stacy L. Leeds, Carolina Academic Press (2019); ISBN No. 978-1-61163-896-7.

*A Guide to Tribal Employment*, by Richard G. McGee, Xlibris Corporation (2008); ISBN No. 978-1-4363-7528-3.

*Tribal Policing: Asserting Sovereignty, Seeking Justice*, by Eileen Luna-Firebauch, The University of Arizona Press (2007); ISBN No. 13: 978-0-8165-2434-1.

*Reservation Capitalism: Economic Development in Indian Country*, by Robert J. Miller, University of Nebraska Press (2012); ISBN No. 978-0-8032-4631-7.

*Tribal Justice: Twenty-Five Years as a Tribal Appellate Justice*, by Frank Pommersheim, Carolina Academic Press (2016); ISBN No. 978-1-61163-665-9.

*Navajo Courts and Navajo Common Law: A Tradition of Tribal Self-Governance*, by Raymond D. Austin, University of Minnesota Press (2009); ISBN No. 978-0-8166-6535-8.

*Ojibway Heritage*, by Basil Johnston, University of Nebraska Press (1990); ISBN No. 0-8032-7572-2.

*Sacred Instructions, Indigenous Wisdom for Living Spirit-Based Change*, by Sherri Mitchell, Esq., North Atlanta Books (2018) ISBN No. 9781623171957.

*Wisdom Lessons: Spirited Guidance from an Ojibwe Great-Grandmother*, by Mary Lyons, Green Fire Press (2018); ISBN No. 9780986198090.

*The Ghost Road: Anishinaabe Responses to Indian Hating*, by Matthew L.M. Fletcher, Fulcrum Publishing (2020); ISBN No. 9781682752333.

*The Manitous, The Supernatural World of the Ojibway*, by Basil

Johnston, Minnesota Historical Society Press (1995); ISBN No. 0-06-017199-5.

*Tribal Criminal Law and Procedure,* by Carrie Garrow and Sarah Deer, Lanham, MD: Rowman & Littlefield (2004); ISBN No. 0-7591-0717-3.

*The Navajo Political Experience, Fourth Edition,* by David E. Wilkins, Rowman & Littlefield (2022). ISBN No. 978-1-4422-2144-4.

*Tribal Administration Handbook: A Guide for Native Nations in the United States,* edited by Rebecca M. Webster, and Joseph Bauerkemper, Makwa Enewed (2022); ISBN No. 9781938065149.


ARTICLES

*American Indian Customary Law in the Modern Courts of American Indian Nations,* by Justice Raymond D. Austin, Wyoming Law Review, Vol. 11, No. 2 (2011).

*Rethinking Customary Law in Tribal Court Jurisprudence,* by Matthew L.M. Fletcher, Michigan Journal of Race & Law, Vol. 13 (2007).

*Key Concepts in the Findings, Definition, and Consideration of Custom Law in Tribal Lawmaking,* by Pat Sekaquaptewa, American Indian Law Review, Vol. 32, No. 2 (2008).

*Good (Native) Governance,* by Angela R. Riley, Columbia Law Review, Vol. 107, No. 5 (2007).

*The Insidious Colonialism of the Conqueror: The Federal Government in Modern Tribal Affairs,* by Matthew L.M. Fletcher, Washington University Journal of Law & Policy, Vol. 19 2005).

*A Legal Practitioner's Guide to Indian and Tribal Law Research,* by Kelly Kunsch, American Indian Law Journal, Vol. 5, Iss. 1 (2017).

*Restatement as Aadizookaan,* by Matthew L.M. Fletcher, Wisconsin Law Review, Vol. 102, No. 9 (2022).

*The Cherokee Tribal Court: Its Origins and Its Place in the American Judicial System,* by the Honorable Bradley Letts, Campbell Law Review, Vol. 43, Iss. 1 (2021).

*Anishinaabe Inaakonigewin: Principles for the Intergenerational Preservation of Mino-Bimaadiziwin,* by Kekek Jason Stark, Montana Law Review, Vol. 82, Issue 2 (2021).

*Indian Courts and Fundamental Fairness: Indian Courts and the Future*

*Revisited,* by Matthew L.M. Fletcher, University of Colorado, Vol. 84, No. 59 (2013).

*Jurisprudence and Recommendations for Tribal Court Authority due to Imposition of U.S. Limitations,* by Angelique EagleWoman (Wambdi A. Was'te Winyan), Mitchell Hamline Law Review, Vol. 47, Iss. 1, Article 10 (2021).

*American Indians, Crime, and the Law,* by Kevin K. Washburn, Michigan Law Review, Vol. 104, No. 4 (2006).

*Toward a Theory of Intertribal and Intratribal Common Law,* by Matthew L.M. Fletcher, Houston Law Review, Vol. 43, No. 3, (2006).

*Looking to the East: The Stories of Modern Indian People and the Development of Tribal Law,* by Matthew L.M. Fletcher, Seattle Journal for Social Justice, Vol. 5, Iss. 1 (2006).

*The Virtues and Vices of Sovereignty,* by Sarah Krakoff, Connecticut Law Review, Vol. 38, No. 4 (2006).

*Tribal Sovereignty in a Post-9/11 World,* by Angela R. Riley, North Dakota Law Review, Vol. 82, No. 3 (2006).

*(Tribal) Sovereignty and Illiberalism,* by Angela R. Riley, California Law Review, Vol. 95, No. 3 (2007).

*Restoring Oklahoma: Justice and the Rule of Law Post-McGirt,* by Sara E. Hill, Tulsa Law Review, Vol. 57, Iss. 3 (2022).

*Digital Economic Zones: A Program for Comprehensive Tribal Economic Sovereignty,* by W. Gregory Guedel, and Philip H. Viles Jr., Tulsa Law Review, Vol. 57, Iss. 3 (2022).

*Lessons Learned, Lessons Forgotten: A Tribal Practitioner's Reading of McGirt and Thoughts on the Road Ahead,* by Stephen H. Greetham, Tulsa Law Review, Vol. 57, Iss. 3 (2022).

*The Rule Against Hearsay, Indigenous Claims and Story-Telling as Testimony in Canadian Courts,* by Zia Akhtar, American Indian Law Journal, Vol. 10, Iss. 2, Art 2 (2022).

*A Watershed Moment: The Health and Economic Impact of Water Sustainability in the Navajo Nation Post Pandemic,* by Onnaedo Nwankwo, American Indian Law Journal, Vol. 10, Iss. 2, Art 3 (2022).

*Extraction of Personal Data: A New Form of Colonialism or Continuation of a Colonial Practice? Adult Native American Adoptees Resist Assimilation and Rebuild Erased Identities*, by Leonard Mukosi, American Indian Law Journal, Vol. 10, Iss. 2, Art 4 (2022).

*Crossing the Dark and Fearful River: Monsanto, PCBs, and Emerging Tort Theories*, by Jamie Hearn, American Indian Law Journal, Vol. 10, Iss. 2, Art 5 (2022).

*Re-Indigenizing Yellowstone*, by Kekek J. Stark, Autumn L. Bernhardt, Monte Mills, Jason A. Robinson, Vol 22, Iss. 2, Art 7, (2022).

*Dispossession: An American Property Law Tradition*, by Sherally Munshi, Indigenous World (2022).

*Lawyering the Indian Child Welfare Act*, by Matthew L.M. Fletcher, and Wenona T. Singel, Michigan Law Review, Vol. 120, No. 8 (2022).


WEBSITES

https://turtletalk.blog

tribal court clearing house: tribal-institute.org

# CHAPTER 3
# HOW TO BECOME LEARNED IN THE TRIBAL GOVERNMENT AND LAWS THAT IMPACT THE ROCKY BOY'S INDIAN RESERVATION. A CLOSER LOOK AT ONE TRIBAL COMMUNITY

## (A) SOCIAL AND HISTORICAL CONTEXT

PRIOR TO 1916. The Pre-Reservation Years, and the Journey to Montana.

Ogimah Ahsniiwin (Chief Rocky Boy) and a small band of Anishinaabe (Ojibwe, or Chippewa) during the journey through North Dakota.

My great-grandfather John Morrissette/Mourisetta Sr. 1849-1932, (aka Oldman Morsette, Indian Scout for the Dakota Territories, and Interpreter to Rocky Boy) (my great-grandfather spoke Anishanaabe, NeIYahw, French, and English) wrote on August 6, 1929 to James H. Hyde, Superintendent of the Turtle Mountain Agency, Belcourt, North Dakota to see if his name and wife are still on record with the Little Shell Band. On August 12, 1929 James H. Hyde replied to Oldman Morsette's letter and stated that "the records of this office do not show that you have been enrolled. Evidently you have been enrolled with Rocky Boy's band and of course could not be enrolled with another band of Indians even though your connection with them could be proved. Accordingly, I regret that there is nothing that this office could do for you in this matter."

Oldman Morsette left his first-wife (Elizabeth Welch Morsette) and their children on the Fort Berthhold Indian Reservation where they would eventually intermarry with the Arikara (Sanish People), and ultimately the Hidatsa and Mandan tribes. Oldman Morsette traveled with Rocky Boy into Montana between 1885 and 1916. Chief Rocky Boy, Oldman Morsette, and Whitford stayed on the Blackfeet Reservation until late 1913, then left to join his group at Great Falls (interviews with Duncan Standing Rock).

The Rocky Boy's Reservation is located in the Bearpaw Mountains with portions extending onto the plains between the mountains and the Milk River in north-central Montana. Historically, the area was part of the large territory north of the Missouri and Musselshell Rivers designated for the Blackfeet Nation in the treaty of 1855. In 1880 the Fort Assiniboine military reservation was established. On disestablishment of the military reservation, Congress on September 16, 1916, set aside a portion of the area for the Rocky Boy's Reservation. Land has been added to the Reservation through both acquisition and reservation since 1916. The Reservation was never allotted. The Reservation is home to over 3000 Tribal members with an annual population growth rate in excess of 3%. The Reservation is in an area of scarce water supply. The region is arid with an average annual precipitation of 12 inches in the area of the Reservation which is suitable for growing hay. Snowpack in the Bearpaw Mountains, which receive an average annual precipitation of 30 inches, contributes to high spring runoff. The two drainages arising on the Reservation are: Big Sandy Creek and its tributaries; and Beaver Creek. Land use in the area is primarily for grazing and growing of hay. Both Creeks flow through Reservation and private farm and ranch land before reaching the Milk River.

## MY PATERNAL FAMILY

My Paternal great-grandparents on my grandfather's side.

1$^{ST}$ family of Fort Berthold, North Dakota.

Great-Grandfather John Morrisette Sr., (1849-1932) (was an Indian Scout for the Dakota Territories, and also Ogimah Ahsniiwin/Chief Rocky Boy's, Interpreter)(my great-grandfather spoke Anishanaabe, NeIYahw, French, and English); married to Elizabeth Welch, Morsette (Wife), Pumpkin Flower/Blossom, a Chippewa Woman. His in-laws were Charlie Welch, and Eaglewoman.

They had four children. (Birth name): Mary Louise Morsette, (government name): Ida Lewis, then Ida Hopkins (born 1874); Fred Fox/Morsette Sr. (born 1876); Carilyn Morsette (died as an infant).

2$^{ND}$ family of Rocky Boy, Montana.

My paternal great-grandparents, on my grandfather's side.

Great-Grandfather, John Morrisette Sr., (1849-1932) (was an Indian Scout for the Dakota Territories, and also Ogimah Ahsniiwin/Chief Rocky Boy's, Interpreter); married to Great-Grandmother, Philommina Sainey (Wife) (1860-unknown).

They had six children.

- Grandpa Joseph Morsette/Mercett (Oct1887 to 3mar1963).
- John Morsette Jr.
- Eiza Morsette Corchran
- Mary Louise Morsette Lewis Hopkins
- Jimmy Morsette
- George Morsette

NOTE: Their land assignment was down below the old dumps (old-dumpsite) lower Box Elder creek on the upper road, in Rocky Boy. Oldman Morsette and his wife are buried in the Agency Cemetery.

My paternal great-grandparents, on my grandmother's side.

Great-Grandfather, Zachary Gardipee; and Great-Grandmother, Cecilia Fayant. NOTE: (brothers: Eli Leonard, and Zachary Gardipee). Great-great grandfather, Boneventure Gardipee.

My paternal grandparents on my father's side.

Joseph David Morsette, (Chippewa/Canadian French); and Ida Catherine Gardipee Morsette, (23 sep 1906 to 10 jun 1996) (enrolled by adoption CCT, 19 mar 1939) (Chippewa/Assiniboine/Gros Ventre/Canadian French). Their land assignment sat between the coulee near haystack road to the east, and between Bonneau dam to the west, and was later sold to Johnny Morsette (the grandson of William "Bill" Morsette Sr.), now where Avis Morsette, and Jimmy "the preacherman" Morsette reside.

## MY MATERNAL FAMILY

My maternal grandfather, on my mother's side.

Michael Henry Gates, (a descendant of the eastern band of Cherokee Indians who were relocated to eastern Oklahoma, known as the "Trail of Tears"). My maternal grandmother on my mother's side is unknown.

## MY PARENTS

My father, James David Morsette (citizen of Rocky Boy's Band of Anishanaabe). His land assignment was the old saw-mill. My siblings and I, and later my children grew up in Duck Creek, and intersecting with what is now called Buffalo Coat Street (the street named for a subchief to Little Bear).

. . .

My mother, Ronda Gates, Morsette (a descendant of the eastern band of Cherokee Indians).

[United States Department of the Interior, Bureau of Indian Affairs, Federal Registry, Chippewa Cree Indians of the Rocky Boy's Reservation, Montana (previously listed as Chippewa-Cree Indians of the Rocky Boy's Reservation, Montana September 7, 1916)]. See 39 Stat. 739 (Pub. Law 64-261).

## 1916 - UNITED STATES CONGRESSIONAL STATUTE

February 11, 1915. 38 Stat. 807 (Public Law 63-244). Chapter 25. An Act authorizing the Secretary of the Interior to survey the lands of the abandoned Fort Assiniboine Military Reservation and open the same to settlement.

**The General Allotment Act and the Rocky Boy's Indian Reservation**

And the said Secretary is authorized, in his discretion, to allot the lands within the reservation hereby created under the provisions of the general allotment Act of February eighth, eighteen hundred and eighty-seven (Twenty-fourth Statutes at Large, page three hundred and eighty-eight), as amended.

All lands are to be held in trust for the exclusive use of the Rocky Boy's Band of Chippewas, and such other homeless Indians in the State of Montana as the Secretary of the Interior may see fit to locate thereon.

Be it enacted by the Senate and House of Representatives of the United States of America in Congress assembled, That the Secretary of the Interior is hereby authorized and directed to immediately cause to be surveyed all of the lands embraced within the limits of the abandoned Fort Assiniboine Military Reservation, in the State of Montana.

September 7, 1916. 39 Stat. 739 (Public Law 64-261). Chapter 452. An Act to amend the Act of February eleventh, nineteen hundred and fifteen (Thirty-eighth Statutes at Large, page eight hundred and seven), providing for the opening of the Fort Assiniboine Military Reservation.

Be it enacted by the Senate and House of Representatives of the United States of America in Congress assembled. That the Act approved February eleventh, nineteen hundred and fifteen (Thirty-eighth Statutes at Large, page eight hundred and seven), entitled "An Act authorizing the Secretary of the Interior to survey the lands of the same to settlement," be, and the same is hereby, amended by the addition thereto of the following sections: "Sec. 10. That fractional townships twenty-eight north, ranges fifteen and sixteen east, and fractional townships twenty-nine north, ranges fourteen and fifteen east, Montana principal meridian, within the boundaries of said reservation, embracing a total area of approximately fifty-six thousand and thirty-five acres, are hereby set apart as a reservation for Rocky Boy's Band of Chippewas, and such other homeless Indians in the State of Montana as the Secretary of the Interior may see fit to locate thereon, and the said Secretary is authorized, in his discretion, to allot the lands within the reservation hereby created under the provisions of the general allotment Act of February eighth, eighteen hundred and eighty-seven (Twenty-fourth Statutes at Large, page three hundred and eighty-eight), as amended.

## 1916-1934

The early years and the birth of local government on the Rocky Boy's Indian Reservation. The Rocky Boy's Indian Reservation is a modern afterthought to the reservation period in what is now Montana.

U.S. Congressional Act of September 7, 1916 (39 Stat. 739) amending the Act of February 11, 1915 (38 Stat. 807).

### The Chieftain System on the Rocky Boy's Indian Reservation

Ogimah Ahsniiwin Chief Rocky Boy's Band of Anishinaabe.

Ogimah Ahsniiwin, is quoted as saying, "Be Kind, and Love One Another."

Ogimah Imsees Chief Little Bear's Band of Nehiyahw; and his subchiefs.

The last Chief, Honorary Chief Daychild.

The Indian Agent/Superintendent/Field Agent.

The Indian Agent, who later became the Superintendent, then the Field Agent, (Jim Montes). Our Indian Agent's duties included, but were NOT limited to: Chief of Police, Chief Judge, delegating duties, jobs, rations, and ensuring that the children attended the day schools, and boarding schools.

Day Schools were in direct violation of the First Amendment to the U.S. Constitution, conducted, and paid for by missionary societies, and implementing Western religious activities.

Day Schools, Boarding Schools, and the Catholic Church, and Lutheran Church on the Rocky Boy's Indian Reservation.

NOTE: The Rocky Boy's Indian Reservation was divided in half by the Indian Agent.

[1] If you lived on the west end of the reservation, you were Catholic by default. The Catholic Church was responsible for educating the children in these day schools that were established on the west-end of the reservation. NOTE: My family lived on the west-end, therefore we were Catholic by default, whether you wanted to be, or not.

[2] If you lived on the east-end of the reservation, you were Lutheran by default. The Lutheran Church was responsible for educating the children in these day schools that were established on the east-end of the reservation.

Boarding Schools, Day Schools (run by missionaries, or ex-U.S. military). They were either military bootcamps, or oppressive religious schools. U.S. Colonial Instruments of Cultural Oppression, Destruction, Assimilation, Cultural Genocide, and Acculturation), and the removal of tribal children on the Rocky Boy's Indian Reservation.

## JANUARY 11, 1870 - POTUS THEODORE ROSEVELT

The military reservation of Fort Shaw, Montana, declared by Executive Order 343B; and embracing an area of about 29,843 acres, has become useless for military purposes. By order of the Secretary of War, the military post of Fort Shaw, MT including the entire reservation, were, under authority of the act of Congress, set aside for Indian school purposes and turned over to the custody and control of the Secretary of the Interior "so long as it may not be required for military occupations."

## 1879-1915. FORT SHAW INDIAN SCHOOL LOCATED IN SUN RIVER VALLEY, MONTANA

Federal Indian Boarding School Initiative Investigation First Report (May 2022), Assistant Secretary – Indian Affairs, Bryan Newland.

Newland is also playing a leading role in the federal Indian boarding school initiative unveiled last June by Department of Interior Secretary, Deb Haaland. The initiative aims to provide an honest, comprehensive review of the troubled legacy of federal boarding school policies, which forcibly pulled thousands of Indigenous children from their tribal communities and relocated them to nearby and far away residential facilities throughout the late 1800s and into the 1900s.

"This report confirms that this boarding school system was part of a twin United States policy: to force assimilation, stripping Indigenous children of their identities, languages, customs, traditions, practices, beliefs, ceremony, and tribal community way of life; through the dispossession of Indigenous lands, and the forced assimilation of Indigenous people."

There were multiple day-schools (half-day religious oppressive schools, and then return to their homes during the week and weekends) that were set up for grade school children around the Rocky Boy's Indian Reservation.

- 1916-1959. The First School House was for grades 1-3, and

was located where the Detox Center is now, as of 1979, and some know it as where the Child Support Division was from 2008-).

- 1918. Agency Day School.
- 1928. Sangrey Day School. This school was run by the Catholic Church. The school was where the modern-day Village Grocery trailers/homes are. NOTE: My father, and his siblings attended the Sangrey Day School.
- 1928. Parker Day School.
- 1930. Haystack Day School.
- 1931. Parker Canyon Day School.
- 1933. Sawmill Day School.
- 1933. Agency Day School. This school was for Sixth, Seventh, and Eighth grades. NOTE: My father attended the Agency Day School.
- 1916-1959. Older students were sent to the boarding schools at Fort Belknap, MT; Fort Kipp, MT; Chemawa, OR; Flandreau, SD for High School, and Pierre, SD for grade school.

NOTE: My grandmother Ida Katherine Gardipee Morsette (born 1906) attended Haskell Institute (formerly called the United States Indian Industrial Training School), in Lawrence, KS.

NOTE: My dad, James David Morsette (born 1939) attended 9TH, 10TH, and 11TH at Flandreau, SD; and attended 12TH Senior Year, at Box Elder, MT (a border town school); and the University of Washington, pre-law (1970s) in Seattle, WA.

NOTE: I, attended public schools in Los Angeles, Long Beach, Riverside, CA; Tacoma, Mount Lake Terrace, Green Lake, White Center, Seattle, WA. Rocky Boy elementary school (7TH and 8TH grades); Box Elder public high school (9TH and 10TH grades); Rocky Boy Tribal high school (11TH grade); voluntarily attended Chemawa Indian School my senior year fall semester, 1985.

I was a member of the cross-country team, I was the second fastest runner, and a member of the team that qualified for the state cross-country meet of Oregon (on my birthday, October 23, 1986). [That was the same date that the boy's cross-country team of Rocky Boy Tribal High School won the boy's state cross-country title of Montana. My brother, Michael David Morsette placed 7$^{TH}$ overall]. I was a member of the boxing club. I was a member of the Indian club drumming and singing; and Graduated from Rocky Boy Tribal high school my senior year, spring semester, 1986.

Haskell Indian Junior College, freshman-year, spring semester, 1987. I was a member of the cross-country team. I was a member of the Indian club drumming/singing. I was a member of the Kansas Army National Guard. U.S. Air Force at Charleston AFB, through Maxwell AFB. Graduated from Stone Child College, Associate Arts, Liberal Arts, (1997-99);

Voluntarily attended University of Great Falls, private Catholic school online, Bachelor of Science, criminal justice law enforcement concentration, University of Great Falls, private Catholic school; Voluntarily attended in person, UGF, Master's Degree in criminal justice administration; Juris Doctorate, University of North Dakota School of Law; Master of Laws, University of Arizona, James E. Rogers College of Law, Indigenous Peoples Law and Policy.

NOTE: I am now teaching courses that I developed at Stone Child College: in-person Summer 2009, Summer 2010, Fall 2010; and now online Summer 2022 – present.

*Tiffany at graduation*

NOTE: My daughter, Tiffany Meiwald. Valedictorian, Box Elder High School (2007); Bachelor of Arts in Creative Writing & two Minors in German and Media Arts from University of Montana (2012); Current Master of Science Candidate at the University of Montana.

NOTE: My son, Antonio "Tony" Joseph Morsette. Valedictorian, Box Elder High School (2012); Bachelor of Arts in Environmental Studies & two Minors in Art Studio and Media Arts from University of Montana (2012); Current Master of Science Candidate in Environment and Sustainability -- Geospatial Data Science Track from the School for Environment and Sustainability, University of Michigan.

He also produces a weekly podcast with his girlfriend, *A Smudge For Your Thoughts*. Episode 2 - Joseph "Ispimikkiew Higheagle" Morsette

Our mission is to promote respect and understanding of Indigenous cultures, by spotlighting perspectives of contemporary Indigenous people.

*Antonio "Tony" Joseph Morsette*

*Antonio at Graduation*

NOTE: My daughter, Justice Dakota Morsette. Graduated from the Cheyenne and Arapaho Tribes Headstart Program (2018). We have since voluntarily enrolled her in the Sacred Heart Catholic School, in El Reno, Oklahoma beginning kindergarten – present.

*Justice Dakota Morsette*

## (B) CONTEMPORARY TRIBAL DOCUMENTS IN A MODERN TRIBAL GOVERNMENT

1934. The Indian Reorganization Act (an opt-in statute) aka the Indian New Deal, or the Wheeler-Howard Act (Senator Burton K. Wheeler I-MT) (see also the Meriam Report of 1928); Constitution; and Corporate Charter on the Rocky Boy's Indian Reservation.

1935-1936. The Rocky Boy's Tribal Reorganization into the Chippewa Cree Tribe as a modern government.

. . .

1935. Section 16. [25 U.S.C. 5123] amended in its entirety by section 101 of Public Law 100-581 (102 Stat. 2938). The Constitution and Bylaws of the Chippewa Cree Indians of the Rocky Boy's Reservation Montana, Approved Nov. 23, 1935.

1936. Section 17. [25 U.S.C. 5124] The Corporate Charter of the Chippewa Cree Tribe of the Rocky Boy's Reservation Montana, Ratified July 25, 1936.

1953. Public Law 280 and the Rocky Boy's Indian Reservation.

The Act violates tribal sovereignty by giving states criminal jurisdiction. The Act is often cited as a rationale for denying PL 280 tribes funding for law enforcement. The Act gives non-tribal law enforcement greater authority on tribal reservations. For example, prior to PL 280, minor crimes committed by American Indian and Alaska Natives were the responsibility of the tribes. Under PL-280, minor crimes can be penalized under state laws as well. Montana is a partial PL-280 State. The Rocky Boy's Indian Reservation is NOT subject to PL-280. There are NO state cross-deputization agreements with the State of Montana, nor its counties, or its municipalities.

1956. The Indian Relocation Act (also known as Public Law 959 Adult Vocational Training Program), and the members of the Rocky Boy's Indian Reservation.

1972. The Revised Constitution and Bylaws of the Chippewa-Cree Tribe, was amended for the 1ST Time. Some of the changes and additions included: established and enumerated the Judicial Branch of Government; removed the lame-duck period for elected tribal council members and judges from six months to one month; removing the ten-year rule; and the one-person, one-vote rule (Business Committee Members are now elected at-large).

. . .

1978. The Indian Child Welfare Act of 1978, [has three components [1] procedural (due process removal hearing (within 48-72 hours) – notice, and a right to be heard, by presenting evidence and witnesses); [2] jurisdictional (domiciled on the reservation (tribal court has exclusive JX over that child), and off the reservation (the presumption is that the state court should transfer that case to tribal court); and [3] substantive (burden of proof, and removal)]; and the members of the Rocky Boy's Indian Reservation.

## Our Family Story, written by me, as told by my biological father

What if the ICWA was already the law of the land in 1970? What impact as a rule of law, would the ICWA have really had on our family circumstances? Could the ICWA had even been applicable? If the answer is yes, then to what extent? How far would the ICWA been able to reach out to the biological mother, to the biological father, to the three Morsette children that were placed in temporary foster care, to the temporary placement foster care family, the Hagen, to the Courts of the State of Washington, to the Department of Social Services, to the Chippewa-Cree Tribe, or to the Cherokee Nation?

*Drum Song for an Indian Child article*

JIM MORSETTE, kneeling right, and his son Joe offer up chants and songs in the King County Courthouse lobby, praying that an Indian friend will be success-ful in regaining custody of the child he had given up for adoption.

P-I PHOTO BY CLYDE KELLER

# Drum Song for an Indian Child

*Photo accompanying the article Drum Song for an Indian Child*

1984. The Establishment of Stone Child College.

I graduated from Stone Child College with an Associate of Arts in Liberal Arts, conferred with distinction May 1999. I was the first Alumnus to graduate with a Juris Doctorate (2009); and an LL.M. (2010). I was honored for my JD at Stone Child College's 25TH Anniversary (2009). I started teaching my own courses summer 2009. I started teaching online courses summer 2022.

## (C) 1986. THE RISE OF FUNDAMENTAL TRIBAL LAWS TO THE PRESENT.

Resolution No. 127-86, to approve the law-and-order code for the Chippewa Cree Tribe, subject to the U.S. Secretary of Interior's approval, Titles I-VII (Nov. 3, 1986).

**Title I, Chapter 1, Section 1.9 – Choice of Law**

"The tribal court and appellate court, in all actions, shall apply the laws, ordinances, customs, and traditions of the Chippewa-Cree Tribe. In the absence of tribal law in civil matters the court may apply laws and regulations of the United States or the State of Montana. When doubt arises as to customs and traditions of the tribe, the tribal court may request the advice of recognized tribal elders."

Some of the tribal kinships and the law on the Rocky Boy's Indian Reservation, that I have attended, and have been an active participant: Sundance, aka Thirst Dance; Sweatlodge; Doorway songs; painted drum; shaking tent; horse dance; give-away; round dance; hand game; pow-wow dancing and singing.

Ordinances, and Resolutions adding to the Comprehensive Law-and-Order Code, subject to approval by the Secretary of the Interior [2004 Revised Constitution and Bylaws, Art. VI, §1(p)].

**The Chippewa-Cree Tribe Recodifying Titles I – XXXIV (see Judicial Branch Website)**

- 1988. The Indian Gaming Regulatory Act, and Rocky Boy.
- 1993. The Interim Compact between the Chippewa-Cree Tribe and the State of Montana, Class III gaming.
- Resolution No. 93, adopting the Chippewa-Cree Tribe Law and Order Code, Title 11, Gaming Ordinance; and can be found not by Resolution No. tracking it, now at "Title XIX Gaming Ordinance, (see Judicial Branch website).
- 1993. The Chippewa-Cree Tribe elected to compact the Bureau of Indian Affairs (FY93) and the Indian Health

Service (FY94) programs under Title IV of the P.L. 93-638
Act. The historical Act allowed Tribes the opportunity to
determine their priorities and to exercise the inherent tribal
sovereignty of the Chippewa-Cree Tribe.

- 1994. The Indian Self-Determination Contract Reform Act of
  1994. Amended the Indian Self-Determination and
  Education Assistance Act to establish within the Department
  of the Interior a program of Tribal Self-Governance. This Act
  authorizes up to twenty additional tribal participants each
  year, and directs the United States Secretary of the Interior to
  enter into annual funding agreements with the governing
  body of each participating tribe.
- 1993-95. The Compact of Self-Governance between the
  Chippewa-Cree Indian Tribe and the United States,
  Amended October 1, 1995 (see also current version as
  authorized by Title II, P.L. 103-413).
- 1997. The Water Rights Compact entered into by the State of
  Montana, the Chippewa-Cree Tribe of the Rocky Boy's
  Indian Reservation, and the United States of America;
  Adopted on February 10, 1997; and amended on February
  21, 1997.
- 1999. Public Law 106-163. The Chippewa-Cree Tribe of the
  Rocky Boy's Reservation Indian Reserved Water Rights
  Settlement and Water Supply Enhancement Act of 1999.
- Chippewa-Cree Tribe Water Code of the Rocky Boy's
  Reservation, Tribal Water Resources Department (TWRD).
- 1999. Resolution No. __, supporting the Economic
  Development Task Force (CCCDC).
- 1999. Resolution No. 111-19, adopting Title 12 – the
  Chippewa-Cree Tribe Environmental Protection Code.
- 2004. The Revised Constitution and Bylaws of the
  Chippewa-Cree Tribe, was amended for the 2ND Time.

## Roadmap of the Constitution

- Article I – Territory

- Article II – Membership
- See Resolution 13-91
- Article III – Organization of Governing Body
- Article IV – Election and Nominations
- Article V – Vacancies, Removal, and Recall
- Article VI – Powers of the Committee
- Article VII – Popular Participation in Government
- Article VIII – Referendum
- Article IX – Tribal Lands
- Article X – Amendments
- Article XI – Rights of Members

Comparing these rights that are codified by the Constitution; alongside the Indian Civil Rights Act of 1968 and its amendments; the United States Ten Bill of Rights; and the Guarantees that are applicable to the States. SCOTUS held that the individual rights protections, which limit federal, and later, state governments, do NOT apply to tribal government. [Talton v. Mayes, 163 U.S. 376 (1896)].

## CONSTITUTION AND BYLAWS OF THE CHIPPEWA CREE INDIANS OF THE ROCKY BOY'S RESERVATION, MONTANA (2004)

Article XI – Rights of Members. In compliance with the Civil Rights Act of 1968 (82 Stat. 77), the Chippewa-Cree Tribe in exercising its powers of self-governance shall NOT;

- [a] Make or enforce any law prohibiting the free exercise of religion, or abridging the freedom of speech, or of the press, or the right of the people peaceably to assemble and to petition for a redress of grievance;
- [b] Violate the right of the people to be secure in their persons, houses, papers and effects against unreasonable search and seizures, nor issue warrants, but upon probable cause, supported by oath or affirmation, and particularity describing the place to be searched and the person or thing to be seized;

- [c] Subject any person for the same offense to be twice put in jeopardy;
- [d] Compel any person in any criminal case to be twice put in jeopardy;
- [e] Take any private property for a public use without just compensation;
- [f] Deny to any person in criminal proceeding the right to a speedy and public trial, to be informed of the nature and cause of the accusations, to be confronted with the witnesses against him, to have compulsory process for obtaining witnesses in his favor, and at his own expense to have the assistance of counsel for his defense;
- [g] Require excessive bail, impose excessive fines, inflict cruel and unusual punishments, and in no event impose for conviction of any one offense any penalty or punishment greater than imprisonment for a term of up to one [1] year/- or a fine of five-thousand ($5,000) dollars or both;
- [h] Deny to any person within its jurisdiction the equal protection of its laws or deprive any person of liberty or property without due process of law.
- [i] Pass any bill of attainder or ex-post facto law; or
- [j] Deny to any person accused of an offense punishable by imprisonment the right, upon request, to a trial by jury of not less than six (6) persons.

## THE INDIAN CIVIL RIGHTS ACT OF 1968, AND ITS AMENDMENTS

- 1986 – Enhanced Sentencing.
- 1991 – Duro-fix.
- 2010 – TLOA provisions.
- 2013-15 VAWA provisions.
- §1301 – Definitions.
- §1302 – Constitutional Rights.
- §1303 – Habeas corpus.
- §1304 – Tribal Jurisdiction over Crimes of Domestic Violence.

## THE UNITED STATES CONSTITUTION, TEN BILL OF RIGHTS

1. Amendment 1 (1791). Religious and political freedom. Congress shall make no law respecting an establishment of religion, or prohibiting the free exercise thereof; or abridging the freedom of speech, or of the press; or the right of the people peaceably to assemble, and to petition the Government for a redress of grievances.

2. Amendment 2 (1791). Right to bear arms. A well-regulated Militia, being necessary to the security of a free State, the right of the people to keep and bear Arms, shall not be infringed.

3. Amendment 3 (1791). Quartering soldiers. No Soldier shall, in time of peace be quartered in any house, without the consent of the Owner, nor in time of war, but in a manner to be prescribed by law.

4. Amendment 4 (1791). Unreasonable searches and seizures. The right of the people to be secure in their persons, houses, papers, and effects, against unreasonable searches and seizures, shall not be violated, and no Warrants shall issue, but upon probable cause, supported by Oath or affirmation, and particularity describing the place to be searched, and the persons or things to be seized.

5. Amendment 5 (1791). Criminal actions-Provisions concerning - Due process of law and just compensation clauses. No person shall be held to answer for a capital, or otherwise infamous crime, unless on a presentation or indictment of a Grand Jury, except in cases arising in the land or naval forces, or in the Militia, when in actual service in time of War or public danger; nor shall any person be subject for the same offense to be twice put in jeopardy of life or limb; nor shall be compelled in any criminal case to be a witness against himself, nor be deprived of life, liberty, or property, without due process of law; nor shall private property be taken for public use, without just compensation.

6. Amendment 6 (1791). Rights of the accused. In all criminal

prosecutions, the accused shall enjoy the right to a speedy and public trial, by an impartial jury of the State and district wherein the crime shall have been committed, which district shall have been previously ascertained by law, and to be informed of the nature and cause of the accusation; to be confronted with the witnesses against him; to have compulsory process for obtaining witnesses in his favor, and to have the Assistance of Counsel for his defense.

7. Amendment 7 (1791). Trial by jury in civil cases. In Suits at common law, where the value in controversy shall exceed twenty dollars, the right of trial by jury shall be preserved, and no fact tried by a jury shall be otherwise re-examined in any Court of the United States, than according to the rules of the common law.

8. Amendment 8 (1791). Bail-Punishment. Excessive bail shall not be required, nor excessive fines imposed, nor cruel and unusual punishments inflicted.

9. Amendment 9 (1791). Rights retained by people. The enumeration in the Constitution, of certain rights, shall not be construed to deny or disparage others retained by the people.

10. Amendment 10 (1791). Powers reserved to states or people. The powers nor delegated to the United States by the Constitution, nor prohibited by it to the States, are reserved to the States respectively, or to the people.

## GUARANTEES APPLICABLE TO THE STATES

[1-8] Limitations on the power of States by the 14 TH Amendment to the U.S. Constitution. The Due Process as sued in the 14 TH Amendment incorporates all of the first Eight Amendments. Article XIV, Section 1. All persons born or naturalized in the United States, and subject to the jurisdiction thereof, are citizens of the United States and of the state wherein they reside. No state shall make or enforce any law which shall abridge the privileges or immunities of citizens of the United States; nor shall any state deprive any person of life, liberty,

or property, without due process of law; nor deny to any person within its jurisdiction the equal protection of the laws. AND see one example of how tribal law, that was enacted on 9/28/2021 can further limit the tribe's sentencing authority, and fines. *See Title III, Chippewa-Cree Tribal Criminal Procedure, Chapter Eight – Post Trial Procedure, I. Sentencing*:

(C) "All persons convicted of any offense may be sentenced to imprisonment, fine, work, restitution or a combination of those punishments. However, no section of this code shall prohibit the judge from imposing any sentence deemed more appropriate than imprisonment, fines, restitution or work, under the circumstances of a particular case. Such sentences may include, but not limited to: commitment to a rehabilitation or alcoholic program, or work for the benefit of the Tribe. Under no circumstances shall fines imposed exceed five hundred dollars ($500), or imprisonment exceed six (6) months for a single offense."


TAKEAWAYS

The 2004 amended Constitution and Bylaws of the Chippewa-Cree Indians of the Rocky Boy's Reservation, limited the tribe's sentencing and fines, because it codified the 1986 provisions of the ICRA – Anti-Drug Abuse Act, PL 99-570, which increased sentencing up from six (6) months to one (1) year and fines up from five-hundred ($500) dollars to five-thousand ($5,000) dollars.

By tribal law, Title III – Criminal Procedures amended the Law-and-Order Code on 9/28/2021, and restricted the tribe's sentencing and fines, to "under no circumstances shall fines imposed exceed five hundred dollars ($500), or imprisonment exceed six (6) months for a single offense." In doing so, the tribe takes a step backward, to the original sentencing limitations imposed upon all tribes, pursuant to the 1968 ICRA provisions.

Possible fix number one. The tribe could amend their Constitution and remove the 1986 ICRA provisions. Tribes do NOT have to codify a federal statute in order to have it applicable, or enforce it.

Possible fix number two. The tribe could amend and revise their

Law-and-Order Code, to meet the statutory provisions pursuant to the ICRA of TLOA (2010), and/-or of VAWA (2013).

Watch, and/-or listen to my interview regarding a codification system, conducted by Monty at StudioOneUND, at the University of North Dakota, Grand Forks, ND on 3/25/2011: "Loyal Tribe Member: Joseph Henry Morsette"

Article XII – Judicial Branch

AND the Constitution grants the Business Committee the power to appoint and contract with the Chief Judge and Associate Judges for the tribal court, and the Chief Appellate Court Judge for the tribal appellate court. *See Article XIII – Judicial Branch, Sections 1 and 2.*

Bylaws.

Certification of Adoption.

Signature, Subject to the approval of the United States Secretary of the Interior;

Delegation signature, subject to the approval of the United States Assistant Secretary of the Interior;

Further delegation signature, subject to the approval of the Rocky Mountain Regional Director, Bureau of Indian Affairs.

The Judicial Commission

- 2006. Judicial Personnel Handbook, Code of Ethics for all court personnel, Chippewa-Cree Tribal Courts, Code of Ethics for court clerks, Judicial Code of Conduct for all Judges, approved by the Judicial Commission; and "supposedly codified under the Chippewa-Cree Tribal Court, under Title 27 – Code of Judicial Conduct Part 1 (delegated and approved by the Business Committee, and established by the Judicial Commission).
- 2007. Northern Winz Hotel and Casino.
- 2008. Title 32, Ordinance No. 03-8 Judicial Commission. The Judicial Commission is the oversight for the Judicial Branch,

made up of five-members appointed by the other enumerated Branch of government (the Business Committee).

## Attorneys, and Lay Advocates

2020. Resolution No. 149-20, Amending Title 34 – Attorney and Lay Advocate Code to incorporate all proposed changes, Attorneys and Lay Advocate Rules, Policies, and Procedures.

## Compare and Contrast

Code of Ethics (Unannotated) for Attorneys Practicing before the Cheyenne and Arapaho Tribes' Courts (2008).

Attorney and Lay Advocate Rules for the Cheyenne and Arapaho Tribes' Courts (1998).

## THE SEPARATION OF POWERS, WITHIN THE CHIPPEWA-CREE TRIBE'S GOVERNMENT.

1935. The Chippewa-Cree Tribe Constitution.

Section 1. The governing body of the Chippewa-Cree Tribe shall be known as the "Business Committee."

Section 2. The Business Committee shall consist of nine members, who shall be known as "Representatives" and chosen from the districts which they represent.

Section 3. Five electoral districts, one at large; and gerrymandering, subject to approval of the voters at the annual election.

Section 4. The Business Committee so organized shall elect from within its own member [1] Chairman, and from within or outside of its own number [2] Secretary, [3] Treasurer, and [4] such other officers and committees as may be deemed necessary. The Business Committee shall determine the term of office for each of these officials and for any other officials or committees that may be appointed.

. . .

1972. The Revised Constitution and Bylaws.

The Judicial Branch was codified into the revised Constitution. The Chief judge and two Associate judges were elected to four-year terms.


2004. The Revised Constitution and Bylaws.

Article III – Organization of Governing Body.

Section 1. The governing body of the Chippewa Cree Tribe shall be known as the "Business Committee."

Section 2. The Business Committee shall consist of eight (8) members and a Chairman all of whom shall be elected on an at-large basis. The Chairman shall file for that particular office.

Section 3. During the first regular meeting following certification of those committee members elected at the biennial election, the Business Committee members shall elect from within its own membership a Vice-Chairman, and such officers and committees as it may deem necessary. The services of a Tribal Secretary-Treasurer shall be available to the committee. Such tribal employees shall be hired on the basis of an employment contract.

Article XI – Rights of Members codified the 1986 ICRA provisions.

Article XI – Judicial Branch was amended, to reflect the Business Committee shall appoint and contract with the Chief Judge and Associate Judge for the tribal court, and the Chief Appellate Court Judge for the tribal appellate court.


2008. Title 32, Ordinance No. 03-08.

The Business Committee established the Judicial Commission and delegated to them the ability to be the oversight commission of the Judicial Branch, including all the Justices, Judges, and Attorneys, Lay Advocates, and court staff.


TAKEAWAYS

The Executive Branch and the Legislative Branch are combined into one branch of government, called the Business Committee.

The Judicial Branch was established by Constitution as a co-equal branch of government, but the justices and judges are appointed and contracted, (rather than elected by the membership over 18), by the other co-equal branch of government, and are also subject to an oversight commission.

What about having a code of ethics for the governing body ("The Business Committee").

What about having a code of ethics for all tribal employees ("The Government").

What about having a code of ethics for all casino employees ("The Gaming").

## COMPARE AND CONTRAST OTHER TRIBAL GOVERNMENTS

- 1937. The Meskwaki Nation Constitution. One branch of government enumerated in the Constitution, called the "Tribal Council."
- 2004. The Tribal Courts were created by Resolution No. 12-2004, subject to repeal by referendum vote by the members 18 and over.
- 1998. The Revised Mescalero Apache Constitution.
- Article XXV, Part III, the Judiciary. Trial and Appellate Court.
- Article XXVI, Composition of the Tribal Courts.
- Section 1. Chief Judge and two associate judges. Appointment by the President and concurrence ¾ of tribal council members.
- Section 2. The tribal council shall sit as a court of appeals whenever necessary and may hear appeals at any regular or special meeting.
- 2004. The Revised Constitution of the Cheyenne and Arapaho Tribes.

Article II – Organization of the Government

Section 1. Sovereignty. The Tribes possess inherent sovereign powers of government by virtue of territorial integrity and democracy. The Constitution of the Tribes shall be the supreme law of the land. All the existing laws of the Tribes shall remain in full force and effect unless such laws are contrary to the terms of this Constitution.

Section 2. Branches of Government. The power of the government shall be divided into four branches: Tribal Council, Legislative, Executive, and Judicial.

Section 3. Separation of Powers. NO official of any branch of Government shall exercise any power granted in this Constitution or properly delegated by law to any other branch of Government except as expressly directed or permitted by this Constitution.

Article V. Tribal Council.

Section 1. The Tribal Council shall be composed of all Members of the Tribes age 18 and older.

Article VI. Legislative Branch.

Section 1. The Legislative Branch shall be comprised of one Legislature. The Legislature shall consist of four Cheyenne Districts and four Arapaho Districts. Each Cheyenne District shall have one Cheyenne Legislator and each Arapaho District shall have one Arapaho Legislator, for a total of eight District Legislators. The Legislature shall select a Speaker form among its members.

Article VII. Executive Branch.

Section 1(a). The Executive Branch shall be comprised of a Governor and Lieutenant Governor. The Lieutenant Governor shall be subordinate to the Governor.

Article VIII. Judicial Branch.

Section 1(a). The Judicial Branch shall be comprised of one Supreme Court, one Trial Court, such other lower courts of special JX as deemed necessary by the Legislature by law, and other forums of special JX for traditional dispute resolution as deemed necessary by the Legislature by law.

Section 2. Selection. Each Judge and Justice shall be selected upon nomination by the Governor, subject to confirmation by the Legislature and approved by the Tribal Council, provided that, if the Legislature fails to approve or disapprove a nominee for Judge or Justice within thirty days of nomination by the Governor, then the nominee shall be deemed confirmed by the Legislature, provided, further that, if the Tribal Council fails to approve or disapprove a nominee who has been confirmed by the Legislature, or who has been deemed confirmed by the Legislature, within sixty days of confirmation by the Legislature, then the Judge or Justice shall be deemed approved by the Tribal Council.

Section 9. Judicial Commission.

(b). Reads in part, "The Judicial Commission shall have the power to make recommendations to the Legislature to remove a Judge or Justice in accordance with this Constitution."

Article X – Sovereign Immunity.

Section 5. Suits Against Judges. Judges and Justices shall be immune from suit in law and equity for actions taken in their official capacity.

Article XII- Removal, Recall, and Vacancies.

Section 3. Impeachment and Removal of a Judge or Justice. The Legislature shall have the power to impeach and remove a Judge or Justice for good cause by a unanimous vote of the Legislature. The process to seek the impeachment and removal of the Judge or Justice shall NOT extend beyond ninety days.

**Preliminary history of the tribal police and the tribal courts, on the Rocky Boy's Indian Reservation**

1916. Chieftain System.
The Indian Agent.
BIA police.
Tribal police.
CFR courts.


1972. The Judicial Branch was codified into the revised Constitution and Bylaws of the Chippewa-Cree Tribe. The Chief judge and two Associate judges were elected to four-year terms.


1982-83. My dad, James David Morsette was the Tribe's prosecutor.


1986. The Chippewa-Cree Tribe Law and Order Code, Titles I through VII, were adopted on November 3, 1986 by the Business Committee, by Resolution 127-86.


FINAL TAKE-AWAYS

Tribal Government and Law in Rocky Boy.

Look at the Federal Statute establishing the Rocky Boy's Indian Reservation (1916).

Look to the Constitution and Bylaws of the Chippewa-Cree Tribe (1935); revised first (1972); revised second (2004).

Look to Article VI – Powers of the Committee, Section 1, subsection (p) to enact ordinances including a comprehensive law and order code, subject to the approval of the Secretary of the Interior governing the conduct of tribal members and providing for maintenance of law and order.

Look to Resolution No. 127-86 enacting the Chippewa-Cree Tribe Law and Order Code adopted on November 3, 1986, subject to the approval of the U.S. Secretary of the Interior.

Look to the Tribe's codes/ordinances/resolutions.

Look to the Tribe's policies and procedures; and/-or promulgated rules.

Look to the Tribe's Judicial Branch.

Look to the highest appellate court, for final court orders that are relevant and on point with any particular issue. NOTE: Example. Tribal court custody proceedings. See Title V – Domestic Relations, Chapter 3. Divorce or Separation, subsection 3.1-3.11. The Appellate Court requires that the tribal [trial] court follow the State of Montana's "Best Interest of the Child Standard."

Look to whether the governing body has delegated some of their duties to an oversight commission and/-or board such as writing codes, policies and procedures (the day-to-day step-by-step operations), and/-or promulgated rules, or court rules to a Commission and/-or Board:

(EX) The five Judicial Commission members are appointed by the Business Committee and delegated the authority by law to be an oversight of the other co-equal branch of government, the Judicial Branch. Tribal Appellate Court. Tribal Trial Court.

## KEY TERMS

- Congressional Statutes
- Ogimah Ahsniiwin, Chief Rocky Boy
- Indian Agent/Superintendent/Field Agent
- Day Schools/Boarding Schools/Catholic Church/Lutheran Church
- The Indian Reorganization Act/Constitution and Bylaws/Corporate Charter
- The Indian Relocation Act
- The Indian Child Welfare Act
- The Comprehensive Law and Order Code/Subject to the approval of the U.S. Secretary of Interior
- Ordinances/Resolutions
- The Gaming Compact, and Tribal Ordinance
- The Self-governance Compact

- The Water Rights Compact
- The Codification System
- The Judicial Commission
- The Attorneys and Lay Advocates Code
- The Separation of Powers in the Chippewa-Cree Tribal government

## A CALL-TO-ACTION GUIDE WITH THE BOOK

**The Quick-Action Steps:**

[momentum builder]; [confidence builder]; [progression]; [personal development]; [a push for action]; and [just do it right now].

1. Write a "why" statement clearly explaining the reason you desire to be a leader, and how you are going to apply it to your life?
2. What is something that you wish somebody would have told you that could have launched you closer and/-or sooner towards your goals?
3. What is your old surviving belief; and what is your new thriving belief you have about yourself?

**Create Your Vision:**

[clarify is specific] [imagine the first-step]; and [remain focused].

1. What are three goals that you want to achieve today?
2. What are three goals that you want to achieve in three months?
3. What are three goals that you want to achieve in six months?
4. What are three goals that you want to achieve in one year?
5. What are three goals that you want to achieve in three years?
6. What are three goals that you want to achieve in five years?
7. What are three goals that you want to achieve in ten years
8. Why are (1-7) a must?

9. What has kept you from changing (1-7) in the past?
10. What needs to change (1-7) now?
11. What are the 1-2 actionable steps that will immediately move your goals (1-7) forward?

**General Questions Posed from reading this chapter:**

1. Give four-ways in which you can relate to this chapter?
2. Research and write a reflection paper on four-different topics found in this chapter.

**Specific Questions Posed from reading this chapter:**

1. How can a person become a member of the Chippewa-Cree Tribe? Explain.
2. Once you become a member, what tribal services can you receive? Explain.
3. How can a non-member Indian get enrolled into the Chippewa-Cree Tribe? Explain.
4. How can a non-Indian get enrolled into the Chippewa-Cree Tribe? Explain.
5. What are the official legal documents of the Chippewa-Cree Tribe, and where can you find them? Explain.
6. What are your fundamental rights as a person, while you are on the Rocky Boy's Indian Reservation, and what legal documents can you look to? Explain.
7. If you as a person, think that your fundamental rights have been violated, where do you go to get relief [the business committee, tribal court, state court, federal court]? Explain.
8. Is there a code of ethics for the Business Committee Members of the Chippewa-Cree Tribe, yes, or no? Explain.
9. Should there be a code of ethics for all (W-2) tribal

government employees, (10-99) contract employees, committee members, board members, and/-or tribal casino employees of the Chippewa-Cree Tribe? Explain.

10. Analyze each of the (1) U.S. federal, (2) State of Montana, and (3) Chippewa-Cree Tribe jurisdiction prosecutorial criminal authority for crimes committed by an INDIAN against an INDIAN on the Rocky Boy's Indian Reservation. Explain.

11. Analyze each of the (1) U.S. federal, (2) State of Montana, and (3) Chippewa-Cree Tribe jurisdiction prosecutorial criminal authority for crimes committed by an INDIAN against a NON-INDIAN on the Rocky Boy's Indian Reservation. Explain.

12. Analyze each of the (1) U.S. federal, (2) State of Montana, and (3) Chippewa-Cree Tribe jurisdiction prosecutorial criminal authority for crimes committed by a NON-INDIAN against an INDIAN on the Rocky Boy's Indian Reservation. Explain.

13. Analyze each of the (1) U.S. federal, (2) State of Montana, and (3) Chippewa-Cree Tribe jurisdiction prosecutorial criminal authority for crimes committed by a NON-INDIAN against a NON-INDIAN on the Rocky Boy's Indian Reservation. Explain.

**The Author's Recommended Readings:**

BOOKS

*Introduction to Tribal Legal Studies, 3rd edition,* by Justin B. Richland and Sarah Deer, Lanham, MD: Rowman & Littlefield, (2016); ISBN No. 978-1-4422-3224-2.

*Tribal Government Today, Politics on Montana Indian Reservations, Revised Edition,* by James J. Lopach, Margery Hunter Brown, and

Richmond L. Clow; University Press of Colorado (1998); ISBN No. 0-87081-477-X.

*The History of the Chippewa Cree of Rocky Boy's Indian Reservation*, by Ed Stamper, Helen Windy Boy, and Ken Morsette.


ARTICLES

*The History of Chief Rocky Boy and His Band and The Founding of Rocky Boy Reservation*, by John Phillip Well-Off-Man, University of Montana ScholarWorks at University of Montana (2007).

*Analysis of the Rocky Boy Reservation's Border Formation 1885 to 1950*, by Brendan Arthur Hoover, University of Montana ScholarWorks at University of Montana (2014).


PODCASTS

A Weekly Podcast - Episode 2 (asmudgeforyourthoughts.com), by KiEwSis, and Sophia.

Podcast by StudioOneUND https://www.youtube.com/watch?v=R6O2akzMu7Y, by Monty.

# ONE LAST MESSAGE

Congratulations!

I am so proud of you for making the great decision to better yourself by reading *Indian Laws Made Easy: Best Kept Secrets Revealed.* I truly admire and respect you for wanting to improve your education, your personal growth, and in life.

My mission with this book was to serve you, and give back to my community. My hope is that you have become more inspired and empowered to think and act differently, BE MORE, DO MORE, and ACHIEVE MORE!

Whether you achieve your dreams and goals is solely up to you. No one can promise, or guarantee what level of success you will achieve. Remember, learned in any particular subject matter is an ongoing process. You should always try and learn something new, each, and every day. YOU CAN begin to accomplish anything you desire.

YOU CAN DO IT, THE TIME TO START IS NOW!

Again, congratulations!

# I WILL LEAVE YOU WITH THESE QUOTES

"Character is what you are, Reputation is what people think you are."
— Henry H. Saunderson. Our dad, placed a plaque on the left side of the wall in our dining room area next to the front door of our house in Duck Creek, Rocky Boy, Montana for all to see and read every time anyone left our house.

"Think Positive, Be Positive, and Positive Things Shall Happen."
— My beautiful wife, Juanita Benally Morsette, (enrolled member of the Ute Mountain Ute Tribe) (descendant of the Dine Nation).

"It all becomes possible once you push yourself through what seems impossible, difficult, and hard! Impossible is only a challenge and should never be mistaken for a time to quit! Embrace the impossible--it's yours to conquer!" — David W. "Famous Dave" Anderson (Choctaw and Ojibwe).

"Indigenous Peoples of Turtle Island decolonize, reengage in ceremony, language, customs, & traditions." Is-pi-mik-ki-ew (High Eagle) (enrolled member of Rocky Boy's Band of Anishanaabe) (descendant of the Cherokee Nation) (Canadian French).

"If I had more time, I would have written a shorter letter." — Mark Twain.

"Insanity is doing the same thing over and over again expecting a different result." — Albert Einstein.

"Everything begins from the mind, including change. So, if you want to alter your life, you have to start with your mindset."
    — Alexi Weaver.

"You never change things by fighting the existing reality. To change something, build a new model that makes the existing model obsolete." — R. Buckminster Fuller.

"It is not as important which action you take, as long as you take action." — Matthew McConaughey.

"Confidence builds and doubt dies when your heart is aligned with your actions. It does not matter where you have come from, it only matters where you are, and where you want to go." — Dean Graziosi

"The road to success is always under construction. It is a progressive course, not an end to be reached. Identify your problems, but give your power and energy to solutions." — Tony Robbins.

Chi-Migwetch; Kitahtahmiin (thank you, very much).

# ACKNOWLEDGMENTS

First, and foremost, Chi-Migwetch/Kitahtahmiin Ki-Si-Mahn-To (I am really thankful very much God, the Creator of us all). I am so grateful to be alive, and fortunate for all the blessings in my life. Looking back over my life, I have been truly blessed.

Second, I want to acknowledge Chi-Migwetch Kitahtahmiin (thank you in Anishanaabe and NeIyahw) Nizhoni (beautiful in Dine) NiChiMos, my wifey, Juanita Benally Morsette for her faith, hope, and love. In my mind, she is my angel. She rushed me to the emergency room on two-separate occasions, and saved my life within an hour of dying both times respectively. She is my honorary registered nurse practitioner that nursed me back to health each, and every day.

Third, I want to acknowledge that it takes a large medical team to help me get well. Therefore, I want to acknowledge all of the Doctors, Nurses, and Staff from Rocky Boy Tribal Health, White Earth Health Center, Meskwaki Nation Health Clinic, Grand Forks VA Clinic, Fargo VA Health Care, Marshalltown VA Clinic, Des Moines VA Medical Center, El Reno Indian Health Services, Clinton Indian Health Service, Yukon Emergency Room, Integris Canadian Valley Hospital, Oklahoma City VA Emergency Room and Health Care and Hospital, Yukon VA Clinic, and Oklahoma University Medical Center Emergency Room, Health Care, and Hospital; and special recognition to Guy Hicks Jr. who was a roommate to me at the OKC VA Hospital, (RIP).

Fourth, it takes a large scholarship team. Therefore, I want to acknowledge that all of this would not have been possible but for the generous scholarships that I had received throughout my seven colleges and universities including: Montgomery GI Bill active duty; Chippewa-Cree Tribe Higher Education Program Scholarship; Stone Child College General Fund, Attendance Incentive, Student Government, Coca-Cola, and Grade Point Average Scholarships; Peggy Nagel Memorial Scholarship; Tribal Academic Bridge Scholarship to the University of Great Falls; USAA Enlisted Association of Montana Scholarship program; American Indian College Fund Scholarship; Margaret Swan Scholarship; Chippewa-Cree Tribe Graduate Higher Education Program Scholarship; Chippewa-Cree Tribe Natural Resource Scholarship; Lewis Oehlert Memorial Law Scholarship; American Indian Graduate Center Fellowship; Indians Into Law Program Scholarship [supported by former U.S. Senator Byron Dorgan (ND-D), and former U.S. Senator Kent Conrad (ND-D)]; and Indigenous Peoples Law and Policy Fellowship and stipend.

Fifth, it takes a large village. Therefore, I want to acknowledge through the years, many have shared ideas, mentoring, collaborating, and support that has impacted my life, each in a different way. It is impossible to thank everyone and I apologize for anyone not listed. Please know, that I appreciate you greatly. Uncle Harold Belmont (RIP) and Auntie Joy Rapada Belmont; Lee Brown; Harrington Luna and his wife; John Trudell (RIP); Vine Deloria (RIP); Auntie Delene Wells; Uncle Ted Gomez Sr. and Auntie Doris Morsette Gomez; first cousin Darrell Gomez; Uncle Victor Morsette and Auntie Elaine Morsette; first cousin Michelle White; first cousin Veronica Marsette McCabe; first cousin Oran Hurst; first cousin Alice Spencer; first cousin Stan Spencer; nephew Sam Pelletier (RIP), his wife Heather, their five children Brad, Samantha, Trevor, Travis, Jesse and their many grandchildren; Uncle Alfred Morsette Sr.; second cousin Alfred Morsette Jr. (RIP); second cousin John Fox Sr.; Uncle Duane and Auntie Bonnie Fox; Father Pete Guthneck; Floyd Benally Sr. (father in law); adopted Uncle John Roddy Sunchild, (Ogimah KiEw); adopted father, Charlie Gopher (RIP); brother Jonathon Gopher; adopted father, Tyrone Gopher (RIP);

brother Duane Gopher; Pau Small Sr. (RIP); Derrek Small; John Gilbert Meyers (RIP); Don Goodvoice; Duane Meyers (RIP); John Edwin Meyers (RIP); Jay Eagleman and cousin Eleanor YellowRobe; second cousin Joeboy and Debbie Healy Morsette; Kermit Morsette and his wife; Richard Rock (RIP); Uncle Tom Gardipee (RIP); Tom Arkinson (RIP); Ken Morsette Sr. (RIP) and Connie Swan Morsette; Duncan Standing Rock (RIP); Russell Standing Rock; Mike and Wanda Parker; Jay and Shelley Vial; Elaine Topsky; cousin Rick Gardipee and Brenda Topsky Gardipee (RIP); Joe Tohonnie Jr. (Haskell Indian Junior College); Dr. Leigh Jeanotte; Arlie Neskahi Haskell, White Eagle; Jonathan Windyboy, Alvin Windyboy, Wesley Windyboy Sr. (Haystack Singers, Rocky Boy); brother Vance Brown (Brown Otter Singers, Meskwaki Nation); brother Alexander Louis Medina, Esq.; Belden Billy; Reggie Wassana, past speaker, current Governor C&A Tribes; Burl Buffalomeat, past Legislator C&A Tribes; brother Kendricks Sleeper, Speaker C&A Tribes; Patrick Spottedwolf past Speaker C&A Tribes; Billie Sutton, past Legislator C&A Tribes; David Christensen, pastor; Evelyn Jimenez, Esq.; brother Frankie Kipp, Seattle Boxing Club; Richard Street; Dan Belcourt, Esq.; Harold Monteau, Esq.; Jay Finch, Esq.; Professor Sarah Deer; Professor Matthew L.M. Fletcher; Professor Robert J. Miller; Professor Rebecca Tsosie; Professor Angelique Wambdi Eaglewoman; Professor Richard G. McGee; Professor Stephen L. Pevar; Heidi Nesbit; Sam Deloria, Esq.; Monique Vondall, Esq.(2004); Trini Contreras, Esq.(2010); Alfred Urbina, Esq.; Belete Tufa Shireraw, Esq.; Professor Grant Christensen, Esq.(2010); M. Brent Leonhard, Esq.; Michelle Lopez, Esq.; Sandra Alicea, Esq.; Sherri Mitchell, Esq. (2010); Sonja Lewis Blake; Dr. Twyla Baker, NHSC College President; Wilma Jean Denny Tyner, Dean of Academics SCC; Walter Echo-Hawk, Esq., President Pawnee Nation; Joseph Plumer, Sr., Esq., and Ramona Plumer; Jessica Bear, Esq.; Larry Yazzie; Ruth Hara; Nicholas Fontana, Esq.; Ben Hoffman; Rebecca Flanders, Esq.; Jackie M. Stebbins, Esq. (2009); Anselma Torres; Pastor David Christensen; and to all of my students past, present, and future at Stone Child College in person (2009-10) and online (2022-present), University of North Dakota School of Law in person (2011), Cameron University in person (2022-present), The University of Tulsa College of Law online

Master of Jurisprudence in Indian Law (2019-2021), with special recognition to William Walton, Esq., and Andrew Tooyak.

Sixth, it takes a large village, continued. Therefore, I want to acknowledge over the years, the Native drum groups that I was honored to have sang with, but are not limited to: Thunderbird singers (where I was first was intrigued by the sounds of native singing and drumming coming from the basement of the Thunderbird House up on Beacon Hill, Seattle, WA; Young Thunderbird Singers (our family drum the original singers were my dad Jim, me, my brother Mike, and my sister Benita); White Eagle singers, Arlie Neskahi; Red Eagle singers (friends of Oklahoma), Max Bear (brother in law); Duck Creek Singers (friends and neighbors of Duck Creek); Haystack singers, Jonathon Windyboy; Southern Cree singers, Harlan Baker-Gopher; Rocky Boy Cree singers, Charlie Gopher (adopted father), Jonathon Gopher (adopted brother); Chippewa-Cree singers, Vern Gardipee (cousin); Eagle Ridge singers, (my four nephews); Mandaree singers older crew (my relatives) and the younger crew; Ree Scout singers (my relatives); Deadgrass Society singers (my relatives); Haskell Indian Junior College singers (classmates during my freshman year of college); Chemawai singers, Chemawa Indian School singers (classmates during my senior year of high school), advisor, Arlie Neskahi; Haskell Indian Junior College drum; Nakoda Lodge singers (friends of Alberta, Canada); Brown Otter singers (friends of Meskwaki Nation), Vance Brown (my adopted brother); River's Edge singers (adopted brothers of the University of North Dakota students); Black Powder (friends of Alberta, Canada); and Sorrel Rider singers (friends of Alberta, Canada).

Seventh, it takes a large village, continued. Therefore, I want to acknowledge through my many years, the outstanding Professors, colleagues, collaborators, and friends that I have had the pleasure to be in their classroom, and/-or office over the years including Rocky Boy Tribal High School: Foursouls, and Nadine Morsette, (oral history, Cree culture, and advanced Cree), Mrs. Parker typing teacher (oldschool typewriters), Kathie Kelly Morsette, (U.S. and American Indian history); Box Elder High School: Thomas Marinkovich, art teacher; Stone Child College: Marilee Russell , Robert Murie, and Steve Galbavy, past SCC President; University of Great Falls: Dr. Cindy Matthews, Deb Kottel, Esq., Steve Nelson, Esq.; Pre-Law Summer Institute (Summer 2001): G. William Rice, Esq, (RIP) (The Four Faces of Indian Law – "All Blow'd Up); Stacy Leeds, Esq., Toby Grossman, Esq. (RIP), John LaVelle, Esq.; University of North Dakota School of Law: ["Have Gavel, Will Travel"], BJ Jones, Esq., Dean Kathryn Rand, Esq., Jim Grijalva, Esq., Keith Richotte, Jr., Esq.; University of North Dakota Dr. Richard Shafer, and Dr. Jill Shafer; James E. Rogers University of Arizona College of Law: Robert A. Williams, Jr., Esq., Raymond D. Austin, Esq., Robert A. Hershey, Esq., S. James Anaya, Esq., James Hopkins, Esq., and Sonja Lewis Blake, co-counsel; Dean, Professor, & Assistant Secretary – Indian Affairs, Kevin K. Washburn, Esq (PLSI Alum).; University of Tulsa, College of Law, Master of Jurisprudence in Indian Law: Assistant Dean Tim L. Thompson, Esq.; Cameron University: Dr. Lance Janda, and Dr. Shaun Calix; and Dr. Carma Corcoran, Director Indian Law Program at Lewis and Clark Law School; James Malinchak, featured on ABC's Hit TV show, "Secret Millionaire," Founder, www.BigMoneySpeaker.com; Dean Graziosi, coach, motivational speaker, and Bestselling Author; Tony Robbins, coach, motivational speaker, and Bestselling Author of "Money: Master the Game"; Jim Edwards coach, and Author of "Copywriting Secrets;" and Jack Canfield, America's #1 Success Coach CEO, the Canfield Training Group, co-creator, #1 New York Times Best-Selling book series "Chicken Soup for the Soul," the Best-Seller "The Success Principles," & featured in the movie "The Secret."

# SPECIAL FREE BONUS GIFTS FOR YOU

## TO HELP YOU TO ACHIEVE MORE SUCCESS, THERE ARE

FREE BONUS RESOURCES for you at:

www.HighEagleLLC.com/free-gifts

Watch, and/-or listen to my interview regarding a codification system, conducted by Monty at StudioOneUND, at the University of North Dakota, Grand Forks, ND on 3/25/2011: "Loyal Tribe Member: Joseph Henry Morsette"

Watch, and / -or listen to my interview on A Smudge For Your Thoughts - A Weekly Podcast, by KiEwSis, and Zosia: Episode 2. Joseph "Ispimikkiew Higheagle" Morsette

Downloadable chart: "The characteristics of criminal jurisdiction in Indian country."

# ABOUT JOSEPH

Joseph Henry Morsette, MSCJA, JD, LL.M., Is-Pi-Mik-Ki-Ew (High Eagle) is a #1 Bestselling author, course-creator, coach, and an inspirational speaker. He is an enrolled member (non-allottee) of Ogimah Ahsniiwin Chief Rocky Boy's Band of Anishinaabe (in English aka Ojibwe or Chippewa) and such other homeless Indians in the State of Montana as the Secretary of the Interior may see fit to locate thereon [see the United States Department of the Interior, Bureau of Indian Affairs, Federal Registry, Chippewa Cree Indians of the Rocky Boy's Reservation, Montana (previously listed as Chippewa Cree Indians of the Rocky Boy's Reservation, Montana)]; descendant of the Cherokee Nation; and Canadian French. Joseph has delivered hundreds of presentations for tribal, and state programs, tribal citizens, high schools, colleges, universities, and law schools throughout the United States, and in Canada. Joseph can speak for groups ranging from one to thousands [in person, and on social media, such as zoom].

www.HighEagleLLC.com

Mr. Morsette has come full-circle, from being the student and graduating from his alma mater, Stone Child College; to continuing to teach, at present online courses, some that he developed from scratch, to researching, and writing his own books. His book series can be used at the other thirty-three tribal colleges and/-or universities; or really any college and/-or university that instructs their students on federal Indian law, tribal law and government, and taking a closer look at the tribal government and laws that impact the Rocky Boy's Indian Reservation. He is the first SCC alumnus to graduate with a Juris Doctorate (JD) (2009); and a Master of Laws (LL.M.) (2010). He was honored for his JD at Stone Child College's 25[TH] Anniversary (2009).

He has formerly taught NAS 253: History of Tribal Government of the Rocky Boy's Indian Reservation (required course); NAS 255: Indian Law (required course); Introduction to Tribal Legal Studies NAS 180 his proposed LS-100 course for SCC; Tribal Courts and Tribal Law NAS 180-02 his proposed LS-120 course for SCC; Criminal Law and Jurisdiction in Indian Country NAS 180-01 his proposed LS 210 course for SCC; Tribal Criminal Law and Procedure NAS 280 his proposed LS 130 course for SCC. He is currently an Adjunct Professor at Cameron University having taught Criminal Psychology. He has formerly taught tribal government (required course), civil jurisdiction in Indian country (elective course) at the University of Tulsa Law School in the online Master of Jurisprudence in Indian Law program; and formerly co-taught federal Indian law with Dean Kathryn Rand at the University of North Dakota School of Law.

Mr. Morsette set out on the educational path in criminal justice, in law, and academia to be best equipped, and prepared for a future career in education and training within his Native community in the field of tribal legal studies, and criminal justice studies.

Mr. Morsette is a Fellowship Award Recipient from the James E. Rogers College of Law University of Arizona, and was conferred a Master of Laws (LL.M.) degree in Indigenous Peoples Law & Policy; conferred a Juris Doctorate (JD) degree from the University of North Dakota School of Law; conferred with distinction a Master of Science in Criminal Justice Administration from the University of Great Falls; conferred a Bachelor of Sciences in Criminal Justice, Law Enforcement Concentration from the University of Great Falls; and conferred with distinction Associate of Arts, in Liberal Arts from Stone Child College.

Mr. Morsette's prior legal and criminal justice employment include:

A Legal Consultant to the Executive Branch of the Cheyenne and Arapaho Tribes; the sole, in-house Legal Consultant to the Sixth-Ninth Legislature, Legislative Branch of the Cheyenne and Arapaho Tribes; Assistant Attorney General to the Sac and Fox Tribe of the Mississippi in Iowa (Meskwaki Nation) Tribal Council; Assistant Tribal prosecutor at Meskwaki Nation; Child Support Tribal Attorney for the Meskwaki Nation; Tribal Chief Judge and Chief Executive Officer (CEO) at Spirit Lake Nation; Tribal Associate Appellate Justice at White Earth Nation; Director of Recruitment and Retention of the Native Americans Into Law (NAIL) Program & the Faculty Fellow, Northern Plains Indian Law Center (NPILC) at the University of North Dakota School of Law; Tribal Associate Judge, and acting Chief Judge at Chippewa-Cree Tribe; Tribal Public Defender at Pascua Yaqui Tribe; Police Officer, Department of the Interior, Bureau of Indian Affairs, Law Enforcement Services; United States Air Force combat veteran of foreign wars (AFSC: 3PO71 Security Police); and United States Army (MOS: 19E trained on the M-48, M-60, and M1-Abraham Tanks).

Mr. Morsette is the Founder, and Owner of "High Eagle Legal Services," see the CCT Tribal Employment Rights Ordinance of (2009), and now "High Eagle Coaching and Consulting Services, LLC" see the State of Oklahoma (2022): Training tribal court personnel, lay advocates, police officers, public officials, staff, and community members; contractual criminal defense; Judge pro tempore; and Adjunct Professor of tribal government, federal Indian law, tribal law and government, and criminal justice in Colleges and Universities online and on campus internationally. Mr. Morsette is the Founder of www.HighEagleLLC.com

Mr. Morsette teaches in the area of federal Indian law; tribal law; tribal government; tribal criminal law and procedure; criminal law and the courts; introduction to tribal legal studies, criminal jurisdiction in Indian country; civil jurisdiction in Indian country; tribal policing; introduction to law enforcement; police theory and practices; patrol operations and procedures; introduction to criminal justice system; field experience in law enforcement; community policing; criminal investigation; corrections and the Bureau of Indian Affairs law enforcement services; Indian Civil Rights Act of 1968 and its amendments; family law in Indian country; criminal evidence and procedure; psychology of criminal behavior; and police management. He is currently in the process of writing a tribal book series for tribal colleges and universities; starting with Stone Child College on the Rocky Boy's Indian Reservation.

www.HighEagleLLC.com
ADDITIONAL RESOURCES
NO-NONSENSE INDIAN LAWS
BEST-KEPT SECRETS REVEALED

AUDIOBOOK MORE YOUR STYLE?
Listen as I Narrate My Book!

To order go to:
www.HighEagleLLC.com

Thank you for your order. Please contact customer support at www.HighEagleLLC.com if you have any questions, comments, and/-or concerns about your order.

**What is your shortcut to success, next steps?**

If you would like to schedule summer courses; fall courses; spring courses; for a keynote and/-or motivational speaking engagements; online courses; one, two, and/-or three-day seminars, and/-or webinars; workshop group training; working with you in a one-on-one coaching program; book signing tours; consulting training; know your rights training; codification training; reviewing and revising tribal constitutional training; reviewing and revising laws, ordinances, acts, and resolutions training; tribal court lay advocate training; Bridge Builder To Success Program and Courses – Certificate of Attendance, Certificate of Achievement, Certificate of Training, and/-or Certificate of Completion Program; Train the Trainer; in-person, and/-or zoom meetings: Mr. Morsette can be reached at www.HighEagleLLC.com

Special FREE Bonus Gifts for You

To help you to achieve more success, there are
FREE BONUS RESOURCES for you at:
www.HighEagleLLC.com / free-gifts

Watch, and/-or listen to my interview regarding a codification system, conducted by Monty at StudioOneUND, at the University of North Dakota, Grand Forks, ND on 3/25/2011: "Loyal Tribe Member: Joseph Henry Morsette"

Watch, and/-or listen to my interview on A Smudge For Your Thoughts - A Weekly Podcast, by KiEwSis, and Zosia: Episode 2. Joseph "Ispimikkiew Higheagle" Morsette

Downloadable chart: "The characteristics of criminal jurisdiction in Indian country."